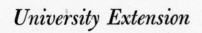

University Extension

THE LIBRARY OF EDUCATION

A Project of The Center for Applied Research in Education, Inc.

G. R. Gottschalk, Director

Categories of Coverage

I	II	III
Curriculum and Teaching	Administration, Organization, and Finance	Psychology for Educators

IV	V	VI
History, Philosophy, and Social Foundations	Professional Skills	Educational Institutions

University Extension

THEODORE J. SHANNON

Dean, University Extension Division
The University of Wisconsin

CLARENCE A. SCHOENFELD, 1918-

Professor of Journalism, Associate
Director, Summer Sessions, Madison Campus
The University of Wisconsin
Assistant to the Chancellor of The University
of Wisconsin Center System

The Center for Applied Research in Education, Inc.
New York

Foreword

When Plato was asked what is the good of education he answered, ". . . that education make good men, and that good men act nobly, and conquer their enemies in battle, because they are good." The enemies of human society are obvious—the threat of arms and anti-democratic ideology; they are also subtle—ignorance, misunderstanding, and complacency.

To combat these enemies we should keep before us the reminder that through education we can develop our human resources and eradicate society's enemies. But we cannot restrict ourselves to the formal education of our youth. We must also engage in continuing education for all our citizens.

Continuing education is one goal of university extension. The extension service—the third function of a university—moves into the world outside the university's geographic boundaries. University resources are made available to as many people as possible with hopes of encouraging and developing each individual to his capacity.

A belief in man's perfectability is basic to our ideal of university education and extension service. The growth of educational services provided by universities since World War II is expression of our belief in the importance of developing an educated populace.

This development is a continuous endeavor. To think that education ends with a certain degree or with the acquisition of a certain skill is a form of self-deception. Education is a life-long process.

"Life-long" education is especially important now and for the future. We are in the midst of rapid changes in technology, population growth, standard of living, increased leisure, and an increased complexity of our institutions. Such a situation calls for new knowledge, skills, and better understanding on the part of all our citizens. Extension education can be the means for providing this knowledge, skill, and understanding.

All those concerned with education will profit from this book by Drs. Shannon and Schoenfeld. They present a well-documented study which is a skillful blending of the history, philosophy, and problems of extension education. Their deep insight into the university extension services along with a readable style make this book a necessary addition to anyone's educational library. It should be read and discussed in the light of current educational needs—and predicted needs for the future. This study announces a new era in university education—the era of the extension services.

H. R. NEVILLE
Provost
Michigan State University

University Extension

Theodore J. Shannon
Clarence A. Schoenfeld

One of the characteristic features of the typical American university in the twentieth century is its extension service, by which the resources of the institution are extended geographically beyond the confines of the campus to serve a widely diversified clientele within the state or region considered as the university's constituent area. Dr. Shannon and Dr. Schoenfeld, in their book on *University Extension,* have reviewed thoroughly the vast range of activities carried on under the name of extension services. They have not only described the scope of these activities, but have also evaluated them critically, carefully balancing the pros and cons currently found in the criticism of these operations. They have also indicated possible lines of development in the near future.

The authors give separate treatment to each of the two main kinds of university extension that have developed in the United States, the so-called general extension, and the agricultural extension carried on under the auspices of the Cooperative Extension Service. The authors point out that, in practically every university carrying on both of these kinds of extension work, the two services are under completely separate jurisdictions. The advantages and disadvantages of this separation are set forth, and the possibilities of a unified service are discussed. In the case of the Cooperative Extension Service, which has been based on the needs of the rural population, the authors lay much stress on the impact of changing social and economic conditions on the older concepts under which the program was organized.

The number of citizens of the United States who have come into some sort of contact with one or more phases of university extension is undoubtedly very large. Probably few of those who have benefitted by the service, however, have an awareness of the vast range of the activities, or of the problems currently faced in continuing to meet the changing needs in an expanding technology. Those who know about "extension work," through only a limited contact with some one or two phases of the service, should find much interest in discovering the broad scope of opportunities that are currently offered. Citizens who have not had previous contact with the extension division of the university serving their area will doubtless be stimulated, by a reading of this book, to inquire about some of the services that might be useful to them and their friends. The sheer description of the range and quality of extension services should leave any citizen with a feeling of pride that modern universities can respond so effectively to the needs of the society that supports them.

The book on *University Extension* fits neatly into the pattern of titles in the Library of Education, particularly among those relating to various phases of higher education. In its treatment of a specialized organization within the broad family of higher education, this book is parallel to others already published in the series, such as *The Professional Schools* by McGlothlin, *The Technical Institute* by Graney, *The Municipal University* by Carlson, *The Smaller Liberal Arts College* by Mayhew, *The Church-Related College* by Wicke, and *State Colleges and Universities* by Wahlquist and Thornton. The volume on *Adult Education* by Verner and Booth treats from a different point of view some of the same problems as this book by Shannon and Schoenfeld, for university extension is adult education administered through an institution of higher learning.

JOHN DALE RUSSELL
Content Editor

Contents

CHAPTER I

The Third Function

Symbiotic relationships between the more abundant life and higher learning have come to be a distinguishing characteristic of American democracy.[1] The founders of the nation saw with Jefferson that ignorance was the enemy of freedom, prosperity, and security; and they set about to erect, sometimes painfully, yet steadily, an educational system that would support the great experiment. As a capstone to that system there have emerged colleges and universities infused with a sense of public purpose.

To their instrumentalities of higher education Americans have brought vital intellectual and financial resources: a profound belief in the importance of the individual, an abiding faith in the efficacy of learning, a goal of equality of educational opportunity, a driving curiosity, insistent demands for both liberal and technical knowledge, and unprecedented public and private support. American colleges and universities, in turn, have come to see it as their mission to develop educational skills unrecognized by the traditional academy, educational resources reflecting the aspirations of a vigorous democracy, and educational services related to the needs of patron communities.

These adjustments have created a new university, still scarcely aware of its powers, self-critical of its limitations, inspiring and inspired in the boundlessness of its dreams. The new American university performs three interdependent functions—teaching, research, and extension. In so doing, the university seeks to be both responsible for traditional ideals and responsive to current public needs.

This text is a description and an analysis of the third university function—university extension.

---

[1] See Alexander Meiklejohn, *The Experimental College* (New York: Harper & Row, Publishers, 1932), p. xi.

1

University Extension Defined

In its broadest sense, university extension is an institutional state of mind which views the university not as a place but as an instrument. Translated into an operational philosophy, extension asks a community of scholars to make itself as useful as possible to the whole of society, or at least to the community from which the institution draws its inspiration and support.[2] In actual operation, university extension leaders seek to identify public problems and public needs, to interpret these concerns to the university, to focus university skills and resources upon them, and thence to translate university insights into educational activities throughout a state or region.[3] Specifically, extension methods may encompass specialized residential instruction, evening classes or colleges, short courses, field research, staff experts on loan to governmental agencies, centers for continuing professional education, exhibits, radio and television programs and stations, off-campus undergraduate installations, area agents, touring orchestras and theater groups, correspondence study, lectures, concerts, newspaper and magazine columns, summer-school seminars, traveling library services, films and other visual aids, conferences and institutes, manuals and bulletins, demonstrations, formal consulting services, and a wide range of informal instructional liaison with individuals, institutions, agencies, and groups.

The extension mission, in essence, is to bring campus and community into fruitful juxtaposition, thereby immeasurably enriching the life of both.

Carried to the ultimate, this definition of extension might seem to encompass the totality of the activities that have become associated with the new university, simply because of the nature of the institution as an unusual concentration of highly specialized knowledge, manpower, and facilities—engaging in public services like hospitals, contract research laboratories, geological and natural history surveys, professional journals, weather bureaus, observatories, museums, experimental farms, and similar agencies. Yet, while it is

---

[2] *Today's Critical Needs and University Extension* (Washington, D.C.: Division of General Extension, American Association of State Universities and Land-Grant Colleges, 1961), p. 1.

[3] L. H. Adolfson, "Extension Theory and Practice," *Proceedings of the National University Extension Association,* 1945, p. 36.

important to consider these public services in the total context of the modern "multiversity," it is not particularly useful to treat them in any technical discussion of university extension. For practical purposes here, university extension is considered as being limited to those forms and types of university outreach which have come to be administered or coordinated by, or closely related to, the two primary organizations employed by universities to carry out the extension function *per se;* namely, "general" extension and "agricultural" extension.

Extension Types

Such a delimitation of university extension should not imply that extension units and their work are identical on every campus. Just the opposite is true. American institutions of higher education vary greatly as a result of differing traditions, circumstances, and leadership. Public educational needs vary from region to region. Hence there is considerable diversity with respect to the nature and scope of the educational services offered to the public by university extension organizations. In general, three viewpoints seem to prevail concerning the essential features of the third university function.[4] The three resulting types of extension are not mutually exclusive. On any given campus the demarcations may be quite blurred, yet each type may be said to have its own "school" of practitioners.

Geographic extension. Sometimes called "extension education" or "extramural work," one type of university extension involves the provision beyond campus walls of some of the credit-bearing educational opportunities, or their approximate equivalents, offered by the university proper, typically by means of off-campus classes, evening classes, correspondence instruction, and radio-television instruction, all aimed primarily at students working toward conventional college degrees.

In this pristine form, university extension is concerned only with the carrying out of the regular curriculum of the institution to a clientele who for one reason or another cannot come to the campus for their education. This concept, while expanding the university or college audience, tends to limit extension offerings to those courses that are currently available in residence, and that can be presented

---

4 Glen Burch, *Challenge to the University* (Chicago: Center for the Study of Liberal Education for Adults, 1961), p. 63.

by instructors who can be spared from the regular regimen. Some proponents of this view would apply also the same academic standards and requirements to off-campus situations as are maintained at home base. Interpreted strictly, this approach releases only a small trickle of the total institutional resources, mostly in the form of classes for academic credits that might be applicable in the pursuit of a collegiate degree. At the same time, this view does accommodate the establishment of branches, extension centers, or evening colleges, whose function it is to duplicate, as faithfully as possible, some portion of the regular program of the parent institution.

Chronological extension.   Sometimes called "continuing education" or "higher adult education," this type of extension involves the selection, provision, and promotion of intellectually demanding educational activities for adults who have completed formal schooling; the curriculum is designed to enhance the quality of individuals as individuals and to increase their effectiveness in their vocations or professions and as citizens of a free society.

Proponents of chronological extension acknowledge the need for lifelong learning on the part of Americans as workers and voters, and accept college and university responsibility for this adult education. Although not wishing to open the doors entirely, such educators permit considerable modification of the resident programs in order to accommodate the nonresident adult. Often this approach leads to a fairly wide variety of educational forms and practices, including conventional classes; occasional lectures; instruction by correspondence, short courses, and institutes; radio and television programs; residential seminars; and other continuing-education configurations. At the same time, proponents of chronological extension urge considerable caution upon extension workers lest the standards of the institution as a whole be diluted. Although they do not insist upon rigorous application of the catalog requirements, course by course and subject by subject, they seek nonetheless to limit the over-all extension effort to those features which are somehow deemed worthy of institutions of higher learning. "College level," whatever that may be, becomes the touchstone which differentiates the appropriate from the inappropriate.

Functional extension.   Encompassing what are called "educational services," "community development," and "applied research," this type of university extension represents the adaptation of university resources to the needs and interests of off-campus youths and adults without regard to age, sex, religion, or previous academic experience; such consultation may be rendered to individuals, groups, organizations, and agencies.

From this comprehensive and vigorous view, university extension is not merely an adjunct activity; it renders the university actively responsible in any field of education or social welfare wherever there is need for revitalization of the old, or a gap or a lack in the new. If service on the broadest basis is the ideal of the university, proponents of functional extension say, then the extension agencies of the university can have no lesser ideal. Theirs is a redefinition of extension from one of extending the university along traditional lines to one of extending knowledge for action to the masses.[5]

Profound consequences issue from this approach. Extension is transformed fundamentally from a passive and dependent agency of transmission to a dynamic instrumentality charged with a special role within the university scheme. Instead of taking its clues exclusively from the established disciplines, it is obliged to step out into the main currents of life, actively seeking among the people to discover and define their problems. The problems, in turn, inspire campus research and determine the extension curriculum and student body.

The Ecology of University Extension

University extension came into being in the first fifteen years of the twentieth century—the product of numerous adult education impulses and a particular American environment. Gaus has pinpointed the critical elements in the ecology of any institution or movement as "people, place, physical technology, social technology, wishes and ideas, catastrophe, and personality."[6] A brief examination of these factors at work in what Morison and Commager call America's "Progressive Era" will illuminate university extension origins and development.[7]

---

[5] Charles R. Van Hise in *Proceedings,* First National University Extension Conference (Madison, Wis., 1915), p. 61.

[6] John Gaus, *Reflections on Public Administration* (University, Ala.: University of Alabama Press, 1947), p. 6.

[7] For a scholarly yet colorful summary of the period, see Samuel Eliot Morison and Henry Steele Commager, *The Growth of the American Republic* (New York: Oxford University Press, Inc., 1930).

People. When Americans turned the calendar page to December 31, 1899, the nation entered not only a new century but a wholly new era. The people themselves were changing. Free schools were producing a citizenry of unprecedented literacy. The extension of the ballot was lending greater vitality and power to the body politic. Millions of immigrants were continuing to come to America, but their institutions, ideas, and cultures no longer flourished as replicas of the Old World. A new environment was fostering an American who was about to make his own contributions to Western civilization, not the least of which was a commitment "to work everlastingly at the task of making learning responsive to the people, and the people responsive to learning."[8]

Place. The frontier was gone. The subsistence farm was going. The 1900 census marked the first time that those employed in industry outnumbered those employed in agriculture. Production farming required new know-how. City living raised a multitude of problems in housing, sanitation, social and racial adjustments, and government.

Physical technology. The world of the one-horse shay was expiring; the world of the bomb was just around the corner. The year 1900 brought the first automobile show to promote the newfangled horseless carriage. There were already a million-and-a-half telephones in use. Mechanization was coming to agriculture. The Wright brothers were getting set to launch an airplane. By 1902 improvement in printing technology permitted a magazine to reach the million mark in circulation. The country was poised on the brink of an explosion in science and engineering that was to demand untold technological skills and transform home and business life.

Social technology. Local government, with its "town meeting" flavor, was finding it increasingly difficult to keep up with the social and political stresses of the time. Perhaps as an antidote, America became in this period a nation of "joiners." Professional, vocational, and social organizations with adult education overtones were looking for individual and collective "improvement" projects. State governors began to project state governments into the texture of American life with social legislation. At the national level, McKinley's assassination and the coming to power of Theodore Roosevelt

---

[8] Burch, *op. cit.,* p. 79.

marked the beginning of the end for a *laissez-faire* Washington, as the federal government took an increasingly active role in American life.

Wishes and ideas. Americans marched exuberantly into the new era, confident that they could make anything, do anything, finance anything, and educate everybody. Nationalism and imperialism came to challenge state's rights and isolationism in politics. Social humanitarianism began to replace individualism as an underlying attitude. Public service began to compete with purely religious impulses as claimant upon the energies of men.[9] There was a general conviction that, as more and more people knew more and more facts about more and more topics, God would all the more surely be in His heaven and all would be even more right with the world. It was the period "of greatest inspiration, of greatest aspiration" in American history. This was the happy American soil in which the seeds of university extension took root.

Catastrophe. Yet, if things had in fact been all right with the world, the flourishing of university extension might have been indefinitely postponed. Actually, the nation was one of sharp contrasts. Millions of immigrants were doing rough and menial work in factories or occupying sod huts on the prairies, while business tycoons lived in grandeur and luxury. Many a municipal government consisted of a corrupt love affair between big business and the big political boss. Muckraking journalists found food adulteration, unscrupulous practices in finance, the rape of natural resources, bureaucracy, child labor, kept newspapers, churches in league with tenements.[10]

Personality. The birth of extension was brought about by an unusual concatenation of educational leaders who shared a vision of a new university that would help lift the life of the nation to higher planes by bringing educational resources to bear on community problems in the spirit of the Progressive Era. C. W. Eliot of Harvard, Woodrow Wilson of Princeton, William Rainey Harper of Chicago, Charles R. Van Hise of Wisconsin, and others began to implement John Bascom's earlier edict that "the university will be per-

---

[9] Freeman Butts, *A Cultural History of Education* (New York: McGraw-Hill Book Company, 1947), p. 440.

[10] Arthur and Lila Weinberg, *The Muckrakers* (New York: Simon and Schuster, Inc., 1961), pp. xiii-xxv.

manently great in the degree in which it understands the conditions of the prosperity and peace of the people, and helps to provide them."

The agenda.   Out of the changing people, places, technology, aspirations, conflicts, and personalities of America at the turn of the century came a new spirit and a new agenda. The spirit was the spirit of social conscience. Its agenda was expressed, fittingly enough, by a university extensionist:

> We live in a progressive, dynamic period, when ideas, ideals, in-
> stitutions, and methods are changing. . . . To live in such a period
> is splendid, but also difficult. . . . The procession of life moves
> fast. . . . To keep step with it requires untiring energy and con-
> tinuous learning. Early education must be supplemented by later
> education. Public leaders in the great social agencies of progress
> must qualify themselves by ceaseless attention and study. . . . (They
> must) find out the causes of poverty, and the way to abolish it; the
> causes of unemployment, and how to readjust the industrial system;
> the conditions which produce physical and moral defectives, and
> how to prevent them; the causes of wealth and monopoly, and how
> to effect a fair distribution of the material resources of welfare; the
> causes of crime, and how to remedy them; the causes of legal in-
> justice, and how to improve both the statutes and their administra-
> tion; the causes of international warfare, and how to overcome
> them.[11]

The Genealogy of University Extension

Yet university extension did not spring full-blown from the head of any campus Zeus. Its antecedents and its midwives were many. As James Creese has aptly pointed out, the history of university extension is remarkably like that of a typical American family, with its roots in eighteenth-century England and the first settlement this side of the Atlantic occurring somewhere between Philadelphia and Baltimore shortly after 1800.[12]

English extension.   In Birmingham, England, as early as 1789, members of a Sunday Society organized regular courses of lectures on mechanics for factory workers, and later put together an artisans'

---

[11] Clyde W. Votaw in *Proceedings,* First National University Extension Conference (Madison, Wis., 1915), p. 314.

[12] James Creese, *The Extension of University Teaching* (New York: American Association of Adult Education, 1941), p. 6.

library. About 1800 a Glasgow teacher organized a "mechanics class" for local machine-shop workers. When he moved to London he formed similar classes there, and out of these grew, in 1823, the London Mechanics Institute. Similar institutions spread rapidly.

British universities thought about getting into the adult-education movement in the 1850's when Lord Arthur Harvey urged them to appoint circuit-riding professors. In 1857 Oxford University introduced a system of local examinations to lend stature to the mechanics' institutes, 300 of which had formed a national union. Ten years later a Cambridge fellow, James Stuart, originated the English university system of extension lectures when he accepted an invitation to make a series of appearances in cities of northern England. By 1908 a crown committee took a look at university extension (the term had been coined in England) and reported that 424,500 students had attended 32,146 lectures in 577 centers.

The American Lyceum.[13]   As in England, the first American adult education impulses stemmed from non-university sources. Mechanics' institutes appeared here almost simultaneously with their inception in England and were greatly stimulated by the moral support of such famous names as Benjamin Franklin and the financial support of such philanthropists as John Lowell, Jr. Prior to 1840, however, it was the American Lyceum that was the real focus of U.S. adult education enterprise. Started by a young Yale graduate, Josiah Holbrook, in 1826 as a lecture system and public forum for the small towns of Massachusetts, the lyceum movement gathered momentum rapidly. By 1839 some 3,000 lycea existed throughout the country, their purpose self-culture, instruction in "rational and useful information," and discussion of current issues. Union officers incarcerated in Richmond during the Civil War even organized a "Libby Lyceum," offering classes in languages, mathematics, physiology, and dialectics.

Public schools.   Perhaps aided and abetted by things said and done in lyceum meetings, the public school concept under the pioneering of Horace Mann gradually acquired popular support and the backing of the courts.[14] By 1860 the American public school,

---

13 See Carl Bode, *The American Lyceum* (New York: Oxford University Press, Inc., 1956).
14 Lyman Bryson, *Adult Education* (New York: American Book Company, 1936), pp. 15–16.

supported by general taxation, released from pauper-school taint, free and open to all, under the direction of representatives of the people, was established permanently in American public policy.[15] It is reasonable to assume that the successful struggle to establish public education for the children and youth of the land was so fruitful and so far-reaching in its influence as to have helped bring about the widespread and rapid acceptance of education for adults.

Farmers' Institutes.   Lycea held in farming communities of Connecticut early took on an agricultural flavor. Immediately after the Civil War a Kansas agricultural society began to sponsor something somewhat similar called a "farmers' institute." The idea caught on around the country. Between 1880 and 1890 farmers' institutes were established on a more or less permanent basis in 26 states, some under the aegis of local clubs, some under state associations, and some under land-grant colleges. A typical institute met for two or three days. Daytime sessions were devoted to lectures and discussions on practical farm problems, the evenings to "culture" and entertainment. Conductors were adjured to "shut off partisan political statements." By 1899 institutes were reported in 47 states, with a total attendance of 500,000 farmers and their wives.

Chautauqua.   Institutes and lycea were to play their part in creating American university extension, but a stronger impetus was supplied by the Chautauqua movement. Take one part each Bible class, circus, political convention, and laboratory seminar, mix thoroughly in a large tent, add a touch of library and a dash of college, bring to a boil over the fires of Utopian planning—and you get a rough idea of Chautauqua. Here was the America of Gladstone, Barnum, Bryan, and Harper blended into a veritable orgy of religious and educational evangelism.

John Heyl Vincent, a Methodist clergyman who later became a bishop of his church, and Louis Miller, a businessman and church worker of Akron, Ohio, started the Chautauqua movement in 1874 when they purchased a camp-meeting ground at Fair Point on Chautauqua Lake, New York, and began a two-week summer conference for Sunday School teachers. Thanks to sound management, astute promotion, and dedicated aspirations, Chautauqua's annual assembly quickly developed a staggering variety of educational work: a sci-

---

[15] Ellwood P. Cubberley, *The History of Education* (Boston: Houghton Mifflin Company, 1920), p. 708.

entific conference, a temperance conference, a church congress, all with an array of secular as well as religious subjects. In effect Chautauqua became a folk university, and college instructors were soon called to give courses on college subjects. The Chautauqua Literary and Scientific Circle, formed in 1878, enrolled as many as 60,000 students at a time for home study and consistent reading. The CLSC reached towns too small to support a lyceum or a library and at one time had enrollments in 10,000 communities in the United States and Canada.

Short courses. Incorporated in Chautauqua was a summer Teachers' Retreat "to benefit secular teachers by combining with the recreative delights of the summer vacation the stimulating and quickening influence of systematic instruction." Harvard University and the Johns Hopkins University had earlier offered summer field trips for science majors. Such innovations led an increasing number of colleges and universities to make their facilities available in summer to special groups, primarily elementary and secondary teachers. The earliest such efforts were frequently not under the direct sponsorship of the institutions, but by the turn of the century more than one hundred colleges and universities had incorporated abbreviated summer terms among their "regular" offerings.

Nor were the winter months barren of special university programs. Land-grant colleges of agriculture began in the 1890's to offer short courses in residence for farm boys who wanted technical know-how but who were unavailable or inadmissible for "regular" terms.

County agents. In what was its first mass public welfare program, the country had had experience with government educational and social-work agents in each county of the South under the ill-fated Freedmen's Bureau during the early days of Reconstruction.[16] Shortly after the turn of the century, such agents again appeared in the South, their work focused on practical agriculture, their sponsors private capital.

Correspondence study. In 1873 an abortive Society to Encourage Students at Home was organized to stimulate formation of home-study groups, prepare reading guides, and carry on regular correspondence with members. The same year Illinois Wesleyan

---

[16] Hodding Carter, *The Angry Scar* (Garden City, N.Y.: Doubleday & Company, Inc., 1959), p. 114.

University undertook systematic nonresident correspondence instruction. At Chautauqua, William Rainey Harper introduced the correspondence study techniques he had first used at the Baptist Theological Seminary at Morgan Park, Ill.

Meanwhile Thomas J. Foster, proprietor and editor of *The Mining Herald* at Shenandoah, Pennsylvania, began to publish a column of questions and answers on mining safety. This led to the development of a course in mining problems. Other related courses followed. The ever-widening curriculum became the basis for the establishment of a commercial enterprise, the International Correspondence School (ICS), a venture which flourishes mightily to this day.[17]

Libraries. With Carnegie philanthropic monies and public funds, more and more cities and even villages had built libraries in the late 1800's. Addressing the American Library Association in 1887, Prof. Herbert B. Adams of the Johns Hopkins University urged the adoption of the English system of university extension in the United States. Public libraries in Buffalo, Chicago, and St. Louis responded. The Philadelphia Society for the Extension of University Teaching, organized in 1890, quickly became the American Society for Extension Lecturing and stimulated the establishment of 23 centers. These centers generally were organizations operating independently of the universities. Typically they were formed by libraries. Lectures on literature, the natural sciences, the social sciences, and a variety of other subjects patterned after English extension were the main form of educational activity.[18]

Lectures. Spurred by all of these activities, a number of American universities in the period 1888–1895 began to offer an English system of extension lectures, with all of its paraphernalia of syllabi, quizzes, and examinations. As a matter of fact, systematic public lectures had been given by some colleges as early as 1816. The program enjoyed a momentary popularity. University presidents encouraged it and leading professors participated. During 1891, 10,000 people took part in Wisconsin and Minnesota alone. But success was short-lived. Administrators waxed unenthusiastic. Pro-

---

[17] W. S. Bittner and H. F. Mallory, *University Teaching by Mail* (New York: The Macmillan Company, 1933).

[18] A. Stephan Stephan, "Backgrounds and Beginnings of University Extension in America," *Harvard Educational Review* (Spring 1948), p. 103.

fessors grew tired, the public disenchanted. In retrospect it can be seen that it was apparently the wrong type of outreach at the wrong place at the wrong time.

Chicago.   At this juncture, in 1892, William Rainey Harper, pirated from Chautauqua by John D. Rockefeller, drew up for their brand-new University of Chicago a "unique and comprehensive plan" by which he hoped to "revolutionize university study in this country." He viewed extension not as a sideline or an afterthought, but as an integral part of university operations, and he set up a Division of University Extension as one of his five coordinate colleges, a Division empowered to offer college courses for college credit by lecture study, class study, or correspondence study. He also put his institution on a four-quarter calendar, thus bringing summer study inextricably into the fold.

The effect of these innovations on the academic world can hardly be overestimated. They gave the concept of university public service its first secure home and its first coherent philosophy. Harper had scattered the seed. It was shortly to find its most fertile soil on the campuses of the emerging state universities.

Public relations.   To mobilize public opinion, Theodore Roosevelt began to exploit the new mass media and to stage national conferences on such critical topics as country life and conservation. Business and industry, pilloried by the muckrakers, retained such men as Ivy Ledbetter Lee in what would now be called "public relations" roles. Even John D. Rockefeller set out to change his "image." The YMCA pioneered organized fund-raising. Colleges set up news bureaus. In this new cacophony of sound and substance, it was natural that public universities particularly would join in the search for devices and functions that would relate impersonal institutions to their constituents. The term "public relations" as such was not to enter the lexicon of university extension until much later, but this is what William Rainey Harper and Charles R. Van Hise were talking about when they said in the early 1900's that "utilizing the opportunity to carry out knowledge to the people will be a practical advantage rather than a disadvantage to the growth of a university along all other lines."

The "Wisconsin Idea."   "In the entire history of university extension," reports Creese, "no event had more critical importance than the establishment of the Extension Division of The University of Wisconsin . . . in 1906–07."[19] In his inaugural address as President of The University of Wisconsin in 1903, Charles R. Van Hise proposed that professors be used as technical experts by the state government. By 1912 nearly fifty men were serving both the University and the state. In 1907 Van Hise asked the State Legislature for a grant of $20,000 for general extension work "under which the University goes out to the people." The resulting University Extension Division was a new agency "by means of which all or any knowledge not only could but would be transmitted to those who sought it or those who ought to have it," as Van Hise described it.

Meanwhile The University of Wisconsin College of Agriculture undertook the expansion of extension programs through resident short courses and off-campus institutes, culminating after 1912 in the creation of county agricultural representatives. On the Letters and Science campus, faculty members manned a summer school that attracted increasing numbers of teachers for refresher work. Other University staff members and alumni assisted a new Legislative Reference Bureau in a unique bill-drafting service.

All these elements—the expert work of professors in energizing legislative reform, the work of the Legislative Reference Bureau, the vigorous general and agricultural extension work of the University, the summer school—were part of the "Wisconsin Idea." Under the leadership of Van Hise and Gov. Robert M. La Follette, and in the halcyon climate of Teddy Roosevelt's America, Wisconsin enjoyed what William B. Hesseltine called a successful wedding of soil and seminar, a fruitful joining of research and reform.[20]

Initial Flourishing

"All through the Union we need to learn the Wisconsin lesson," Theodore Roosevelt said. The lesson was learned. By 1914 some 30 universities had organized full-blown general extension divisions, and 25 agricultural colleges were actively engaged in extension work.

Although called university extension, and organized in part to

---

[19] Creese, *op. cit.*, p. 98.

[20] For a more detailed analysis, see Vernon Carstensen, "The Origin and Early Development of the Wisconsin Idea," *Wisconsin Magazine of History* (Spring 1956), pp. 181–88.

give university credit, only a small portion of the work was actually along conventional university lines. Indeed, extension early became, at its best, a people's university, offering utilitarian information at virtually any level. Consciously patterned as much after public and private action-agencies as after "English" extension, aimed at being all things to all men, evangelical in outlook, unreservedly committed to the assumption that one sure way to earthly salvation was through education, university extension developed quickly, energetically, and conspicuously.

The typical agricultural extension service aimed at posting an agent in each county. The typical general extension division consisted of four departments: correspondence study, instruction by lectures, debating and public discussion, and general information and welfare. States were divided into districts, field organizations were created, and peripatetic professors were put on the road. Textbooks were written to meet the specific needs of the artisans who made up the bulk of the enrollments. The success of the experiment was reflected in quickly increased interest and support.

Assembled for the first time together in 1915, the pioneer extensionists agreed that "university extension work (has as its purpose) to carry the best knowledge and the best methods to the people, to develop the social impulse and judgment, to bring about the kind and amount of activity which will meet the countless and the complex needs of 20th century civilization."[21]

This was not the passive transmission of traditions nor even the antiseptic inculcation of practical know-how; it was education for action—curriculums and devices shaped to meet the needs of the day as the university perceived them. This was modern university extension. It was indeed, as Van Hise said, "a new thing in the world."

No longer were colleges and universities to confine their work within their own walls. More and more they attempted to reach all the people of the communities to which they ministered. The campus of the state university came to be coextensive with the borders of the state whose people were taxed for its support. The great universities with large endowments attempted to serve still larger areas. "Wherever men and women labored in the heat, or toiled in the

---

21 Votaw, *op. cit.*, p. 314.

shadows, in field or forest, or mill or shop or mine, in legislative halls
or executive offices, in society or in the home, at any task requiring
an exact knowledge of facts, principles, or laws, there the university
came to see both its duty and its opportunity."[22]

University Extension Today

Almost all American institutions of higher learning today attempt
to offer some services to the general public over and above that
which is thought of as conventional collegiate instruction. About
such activities it is extremely difficult to generalize, for a number
of reasons. First, as previously stated, American colleges and universities vary greatly in their traditions, circumstances, and aspirations.
Second, by its very nature as an institution's primary mechanism of
response to environmental stresses and needs, extension itself varies
from campus to campus and contributes in turn to institutional differences. To speak, then, of a university extension standard and to
seek a pattern of extension uniformity are to pursue contradictions
in terms. But some synthesis is possible.

Broad base.   By no means has extension been limited to the
public institutions of higher education. Some of the earliest notable
programs, both formal and informal, were undertaken by the *private*
colleges. Today many of these colleges and universities have a strong
commitment to public service of the highest quality. While it would
seem unreasonable to expect such institutions to assume the breadth
of responsibilities appropriate to public counterparts, many have
nonetheless manifested considerable enterprise in both geographic
outreach and program diversity.

Five main types of institutions should be distinguished in any
review of *public* institutions of higher learning and their extension
programs: the separated state universities, the land-grant colleges
and universities, the combined land-grant colleges and state universities, state colleges (including teachers' colleges), and municipal
universities. Considerable flux is evident in the organization, administration, and scope of these institutions as they reshape themselves
to cope with the changing educational requirements of their milieu.

---

[22] P. P. Claxton, "Letter of Transmittal," *University Extension in the United
States,* Bulletin No. 592, Louis E. Reber (ed.) (Washington, D.C.: United States
Bureau of Education, 1914), p. 4.

As a consequence, it is particularly difficult to delineate their extension responsibilities with precision.

Prior to this period of transmutation, a rough differentiation could be discerned. In general, the separated state universities, through schools and departments of the university or through a so-called general extension division, attempted to extend the fields of study represented in their particular institutions. The land-grant colleges were responsible primarily for extension in agriculture, home economics, sometimes engineering, and related fields, effected through the Cooperative Extension Service, a tripartite agency supported by the United States Department of Agriculture, the respective states, and local instrumentalities. In the combined universities, where functional extension is employed on a massive scale, rather than have combined agencies as might seem reasonable, two separate extension mechanisms tended to exist side by side with little or no significant intercourse between them. The state colleges concentrated almost exclusively upon services related to the needs of public schools, particularly in-service teacher education. Municipal universities concentrated on evening college work and services to business and industry.

Broad coordination. Several national organizations have been formed to coordinate, clarify, and give impetus to university extension efforts. Chief among these are the National University Extension Association, the Association of University Evening Colleges, the Association of State Universities and Land-Grant Colleges, and the (Cooperative) Extension Committee on Organization and Policy (ECOP). Special professional associations also concern themselves with the problems of university-related programs of continuing education, notable among these being the Adult Education Association, USA.

Broad outreach. Hazardous as it is to categorize the configurations of university extension, it is even more hazardous to estimate its output. There are no comprehensive, cohesive "enrollment" or "contact" reports compiled by any agency.

Those institutions affiliated with the Association of University Evening Colleges and the National University Extension Association have begun to keep fairly systematic enrollment statistics on their more formal types of general extension instruction. Their figures for 1962–63 were as follows:

Extension class students	1,302,148
Correspondence students	167,690
Conference and institute students	1,095,264
Discussion group students	47,448[23]

Although there are undoubtedly some duplications in these figures, they total 2,612,550, and this compares very closely with the figure of 2,640,000 arrived at by the National Opinion Research Center of the University of Chicago as "the estimated number of different persons who attended classes, lectures, talks, or discussion groups" sponsored by colleges and universities in 1963.[24]

On the basis of these data, it could be estimated that American colleges and universities enrolled on the order of three million adults in more or less systematic forms of extension teaching in 1965.

The less formal types of extension liaison are much more difficult to document. Agricultural extension reports say that Cooperative Extension workers are currently contacting, "with varying degrees of intensity," about ten million people each year.[25] Morton stated ten years ago that general extension services were being utilized in some way by "over fifty million people."[26] Whether these figures are inflated or conservative, it is almost impossible to say. Even if the figures are cut in half, one can say that "university extension draws more adults than baseball."[27]

From another perspective, the money budgeted by colleges and universities is an indication of the extent of the extension enterprise. Pyle estimated that 72 NUEA institutions alone in 1962 earmarked over $50 million for general extension activities.[28] Land-grant colleges and universities budgeted nearly $178 million in 1964 for agricultural extension. These figures are undoubtedly increasing annually.

---

[23] "Enrollment Statistics for the Fiscal Year 1962–63," *Joint Report, AUEC–NUEA* (Los Angeles: University of California at Los Angeles, 1963), p. 4.

[24] *Volunteers for Learning* (Chicago: National Opinion Research Center, University of Chicago, 1963), p. 3.

[25] *"Scope Report"* (Washington, D.C.: American Association of State Universities and Land-Grant Colleges, April, 1958), p. 3.

[26] John R. Morton, *University Extension in the United States* (University, Ala.: University of Alabama Press, 1953), p. 134.

[27] *Volunteers for Learning*, p. 25.

[28] H. G. Pyle, "Response to Questions Raised in Connection with Proposed University Extension Bill" (University Park, Pa.: The Pennsylvania State University, July 1, 1963), p. 7. Mimeograph.

Staff size is another index of extension scope. Knowles put the combined figure of adult education workers in agricultural and general extension at over 13,000 full-time and nearly 1,190,000 part-time in 1955.[29] Again, these figures certainly are higher now.

Unquestionably, by any quantitative criterion, university extension is a going concern.

Objectives and Objections

Certain common aims have prevailed among universities in the country from the beginning of the extension movement. The principal aim has been to make university resources available and useful to as many people as possible. Correlatively the aim has been to encourage and help every individual to develop himself to the extent of his capacity. Implicit in these aims are a basic belief in man's perfectability and a faith in his ability to solve his problems peaceably through the intervention of mind and the application of intelligence.

It would be a mistake, however, to assume that only such lofty generalities inspired the early extension educator. Compelling as these sanguine ideals might have seemed, also motivating him were the tangible, practical, workaday requirements of a developing society experimenting with large-scale political democracy while undergoing rapid industrialization.

Whether moved by liberal ideals concerning the nature of man or by the press of mundane affairs, the prescription of the early educator was one and the same: the application of knowledge. To him the widespread diffusion and application of knowledge (or the "socialization" of knowledge, as it was expressed at the turn of the century) was both imperative and urgent. This sense of urgency and necessity is reflected in the literature of the extension movement of the period, as is the ambivalence between the idealistic and the practical. To this day, indeed, some of the original zeal still permeates the movement, though the earlier preoccupation with philosophy and rationale appears to have given way to bureaucratic and operational considerations. So, too, has persisted the dichotomy

---

[29] Malcolm S. Knowles, "Adult Education in the United States," *Adult Education* (Winter 1955), p. 76.

between the liberal and the pragmatic, both of which are represented amply in modern-day extension practices.

No less than their latter-day counterparts, appalled by the vision of impending crisis in higher education under the impact of swollen enrollments and rising research responsibilities, some earlier spokesmen for both faculty and administration questioned the wisdom of obligating universities with the additional burdensome function of direct educational services to the public at large. Granted the need for continuing education, why, they asked, was the university uniquely qualified for this work? Were not other agencies more appropriate to the task?

While this questioning attitude was certainly widely prevalent, so, too, were responses forthcoming from supporters of the movement, both inside and outside the university. Responsible spokesmen for university extension have always maintained it to be essential for the university to supplement, not supplant, the work of other organized institutions and agencies concerned with education. Wherever these agencies were adequately discharging their educational duties, it was improper for the university to intrude. Rather, it was necessary that the university inspire, stimulate, and train others to improve their capacities for educating the public, including the adult public. More than that, in some instances it might be appropriate for the university actually to assist in the creation of agencies and associations designed to further the extension concept.

From the moment of its inception down to the present, there have been those who say extension leads to a lowering of dignity and a dissipation of energy on the part of the prostitute institution. Functional university extension, particularly, has been termed "substandard" or "noneducational" or even "anti-university." One of Willa Cather's professors resisted bitterly what he called "the new commercialism—the aim to 'show results' that undermines and vulgarizes education." Others of like mind said extension was "largely organized and operated on very thin material; wind and water have had too much to do with it." Henry M. Wriston has linked "the engulfment of the arts" to the rise of the service university. Cyril Houle criticizes extension's "public relations" overtones.

On the other side, many have agreed with Claxton that "there is no dignity to compare with the dignity of service; the only way to conserve and increase strength is to spend it wisely." James E.

Conant's current assessment is unequivocal: "The essential motivating force behind a university's work in all times and places when universities have flourished has been the connection between the scholar's activities and the burning questions of the day."[30]

At its best today, university extension has become generally recognized as an intimate, essential, and honorable aspect of the total enterprise of the modern American university. American adults turn to many educational and public service agencies to meet their needs. Increasingly they are turning to the university. This is natural, because many aspects of education for adult action can be provided best by the university, with its specialized knowledge, its research interests and facilities, its teaching skills, its organizing capacity, its prestige, and its commitment to extension. Thus there emerges a major third university function, a role in which the campus will, freely and without perversion, lend its knowledge and skills to all the people in their communities and regions for the solution of the everyday problems of living and for the intellectual and spiritual enrichment of their lives.[31]

The true university, it has been said, should have "both open gates and cloistered libraries; both practical, itinerant messengers and theoretical, isolated scholars."[32] It is given to university extension to provide the missionaries, who have extended the boundaries of the campus and have brought back to the campus the problems and aspirations of the people.

---

[30] Quoted by Paul F. Douglas in "Conant's Concept of University Administration," *Journal of Higher Education* (February 1954), p. 63.

[31] L. H. Adolfson, "University Extension in the Years Ahead," (Madison, Wis., 1953), p. 4. Mimeograph.

[32] Claxton, *op. cit.*, p. 3.

CHAPTER II

General Extension

The face of the American renaissance called adult education is vividly visible. It has reached perhaps the height of its vigor in California, mostly because there exists there the University of California Extension.... (Its students) gather in living rooms and lecture halls. They come to hear about politics and sociology, communism and capitalism, tapestry and astrodynamics, architecture and archaeology, art and Oriental music, mathematics and semantics. They sit under the cool pines on a California mountaintop to discuss great issues. They sit in a darkened theater to watch plays they never heard of or to view obscure but artful foreign films they never saw before. They gather 200,000 strong each year. They convene in Los Angeles and San Diego and Riverside and Anaheim and in 170 other locations in California. Or they correspond from many states in the union.... (Thus has the) University of California assumed a third function, ... "participating in the area of public responsibility," ... "wielding a catalytic influence in the community," ... "addressing and trying to solve the pressing problems of the 20th century."[1]

This is university general extension in action in the sixties. The general extension arm of the University of California is the largest such organization in the world, and hence its range of curriculums and clientele is unusually wide, but something of the same spirit, if not the same scope, is at work in the patron communities or regions of many other American colleges and universities today.

To effect this outreach, the typical college and university designates a chief extension administrative officer and puts him in charge of a special unit. The officer is variously called "dean," "director," "coordinator," or even "vice-president" of "extension," "university extension," "general extension," "continuing education," "adult education," "public service," or "educational services." His unit may be called a "division," "center," "office," "bureau," or "university college." Probably the most common nomenclature is "dean of the university extension division." For various reasons, not all of them

---

[1] John C. Waugh, *The Christian Science Monitor* (March 14, 1962).

logical, some forms of university outreach will probably not be under the domain of this instrumentality. By and large, however, university general extension configurations, with a common core of purpose and practice, have been established as major units of enough institutions to make it possible to generalize about their organization, functions, devices, facilities, personnel, clientele, and curriculums.

But before such generalizations are made, it will be instructive to review quickly the ladder up which university general extension has climbed since the early 1900's.

Historical Highlights

Nothing in American history has been more striking, historian Frederick Jackson Turner observed, than "the steady pressure of democracy upon its universities to adapt them to the requirements of all the people." As a primary vehicle of that adjustment, university general extension has been profoundly influenced by fundamental tides and stresses at work upon the American people. Hence any account of extension's history since its initial flourishing is inevitably punctuated by famous headlines.

World War I. Virtually overnight in 1917 university general extension doffed its civilian garb and left its state or regional orientations to join the national effort. Special correspondence courses were written for soldiers and sailors. Red Cross nursing classes were offered. Post-graduate medical refresher training entered extension's curriculum. From extension's presses came bulletins on such topics as food conservation, women in industry, and fuel conservation. Package libraries on "causes of the Great War" made their contribution to anti-German propaganda. Extension leaders went on leave to supervise special training schools set up by the Emergency Fleet Corporation and to take charge of the American Expeditionary Force University in France.

The twenties. After their emotional binge in World War I, Americans were "tired, irritable, disputatious, prone to let their responsibilities go, prone to show their pent-up annoyance with people with whom they had to work cheerfully in wartime, . . . prone to indulge in feverish relaxations," and prone to believe, as F. Scott Fitzgerald was to phrase it, that "all gods [were] dead, all wars fought, all faiths in man shaken."[2] This was a far cry from the American temper that had fostered university extension.

Faced with an inhospitable climate, general extension turned inward on itself in a number of ways. It became less a movement and more a cult, and like all cults it became more concerned with how it did things than what it did. The new National University Extension Association devoted much time to "the standards of university extension credit courses," and adopted an "official nomenclature" spelling out minutely what the various titles in the extension hierarchy should be. As W. S. Bittner was to observe, "now there is nothing significantly new," other than limited utilization of radio as an extension medium.

Depression. The reverberations of the 1929 economic crash were detected quickly and plainly by extensionists, and emergency extension programs antedated the New Deal by a good two years. There were off-campus classes for high school graduates who couldn't afford to go away to college, special correspondence courses for the unemployed, and package libraries on refinancing mortgages and similar topics. Some states provided extension scholarships for the indigent. With the advent of another Roosevelt, extension once again came into its own. University professors took off for Washington to take their places in a "brain trust" of presidential advisers, and federal funds came to the campus to stimulate extension activities: correspondence courses for boys in Civilian Conservation Corps (CCC) camps; vocational rehabilitation classes under the Social Security Act; projects in workers' education, adult education, and citizenship education under Works Projects Administration (WPA); projects for unemployed youths under National Youth Administration (NYA); new buildings financed by Public Works Administration (PWA); pilot training under Civil Aeronautics Administration (CAA).

Extension was beginning to "move toward a fuller realization of earlier dreams, that a university with its extraordinary equipment and its congregation of teachers and scholars would consider and provide for the part-time adult student" and even more, would "take the university—the professors, the books, the skills, the findings of

---

[2] For a brilliant portrait of the twenties, see Frederick Lewis Allen, *Only Yesterday* (New York and London: Harper & Row, Publishers, 1931).

research, the interpretations, the insights, the forums, the publications—to the people" . . . "for the economic betterment, the intellectual stimulation, and the spiritual enrichment of their lives."

World War II. University general extension went to war early. It recruited money, men, and mission in 1940. The money came through the United States Office of Education—millions for emergency manpower training. The men—and women—came from all walks of life; in just one year, 900,000 people had gone through the courses. The mission was that combination of fear, high strategy, imperialism, and missionary zeal which Henry R. Luce was to call "The American Century." The crash of bombs at Pearl Harbor turned the university into more of a camp than a campus, and it was to general extension that presidents and generals looked for know-how in operating special training programs for many types of uniformed personnel and in promoting all manner of home-front "drives." Extensionists themselves marched off to man the mushrooming bureaus in Washington or machine guns at Anzio and Luzon. The new United States Armed Forces Institute, a mammoth correspondence-study college, drew on extension experience and added to extension prestige. Continuing Engineering, Science, Manpower War Training (ESMWT) programs introduced laborers to university outreach. Businessmen turned to extension for help in forwarding the work of their Committee for Economic Development.

Postwar years. The marriage between university extension and national defense was to have profound implications for the postwar years. A country that had always had a deep-seated belief in the efficacy of higher learning suddenly found new and dramatic evidence to buttress that faith. The flood of veterans to the campus in 1946–47 was merely symptomatic of a broad American thirst for knowledge and a deep national conviction that knowledge was power. That thirst and that conviction were to provide the stimulus for a new flourishing of functional university extension.

Assembled in 1962 to observe the centennial of the land-grant college movement, members of the National University Extension Association expressed satisfaction with the record of general extension, but recognized that past accomplishments were merely prelude to future responsibilities. We must work as never before, they agreed, "to facilitate . . . the dissemination of university findings, skills, methods, and standards to all who can use them, (because) the release of human potentialities may well be the *sine qua non* for the preservation of our way of life."[3]

Organization

Ideally one might suppose that if a spirit of public service permeated a faculty as do commitments to conventional instruction and scholarly investigation, a special extension unit would be unnecessary. Suffice it to say there is little evidence that extension in adequate depth and breadth can emerge where there is no division specifically charged to direct it; the roles of stimulation, coordination, management, and continuity, which extension divisions contribute, are crucial to successful extension programs.

Responsibilities. In their organizational patterns university general extension divisions are characterized by a lack of uniformity. In general extension operations of most any structure, however, provision will be made for accomplishment of the following responsibilities:

1. Executive management—broad planning, supervision, fiscal control, rendering of reports, and particularly, personnel relations.
2. Administrative support—accounting, registration, recording, stenographic and clerical services, publicity, and so on.
3. Instruction—including the gamut of informal consultative relationships as well as the more formal types of teaching.
4. Program development, promotion, and evaluation—determining the interests and needs of clientele and the arrangements by which they are willing and able to utilize university resources effectively.
5. Liaison—with campus colleges, schools, departments, offices, and faculty members; and with off-campus individuals, groups, organizations, and agencies.
6. Instructional resources—duplicating, printing, editing, tests, audio-visual materials, library services, programmed materials, electronic devices—the ever-increasing technology of learning.
7. Logistics—management of facilities, stocking of supplies, fiscal control.
8. Applied research—surveys, field investigations, and so on, concerning public problems.
9. Institutional studies—self-analyses, formal or informal, designed to reveal or inspire ways of improving extension operations.

[3] *Report of the Policy Statement Committee* (Washington, D.C.: The National University Extension Association, n.d.), p. 20.

10. Basic research—fundamental investigations, principally in the areas of psychology, sociology, and education, designed primarily to explore the phenomena of adult learning.

Patterns. While these extension responsibilities will be assigned, explicitly or implicitly, to someone or some groups in the typical university, the "tables of organization" will vary markedly from campus to campus. For example, some universities have built virtually self-contained extension arms, with all or most campus disciplines and services represented by full-time personnel within the division. At the other extreme, some universities favor an extremely lean extension organization, composed essentially of administrative personnel, with the bulk of the functions performed on an *ad hoc* basis by people outside the division. Other institutions effect a variety of compromises, characterized by "split appointments," advisory committees, and consultants. Even within the extension division an ambivalence in the approach to organization is frequently apparent. For instance, some bureaus will represent methods of instruction—eg., correspondence study; other parallel bureaus will represent an academic discipline—eg., world affairs; others, a clientele focus—eg., women's programs; and still others will represent a blend—eg., radio services to schools. When extension deans get together it is little wonder that they frequently spend time trying to unravel each other's charts of organization!

This absence of uniformity in general extension organization is understandable. Universities themselves differ in organization. Extension deans have differing approaches to administration. Universities and their extension divisions tend to select out of the total public service spectrum those functions that befit particular traditions, resources, and priorities. Further, the general extension movement is young, as educational movements go. It has developed at dispersed sites, in response to varying circumstances, in the absence of any federal funds that might have imposed a sameness, and without much systematic theory that could have lent philosophic guidelines. Yet everywhere it has generally withstood that most pragmatic of tests: it *has* worked and *is* working. In fact, the very flexibility of extension organization has been one of its great strengths. Whether so eclectic an approach can continue to render a sound account of itself remains to be seen.

Functions

In seeking to accomplish its overall mission of transmitting university skills and resources widely in usable form, university general extension typically finds itself engaged in a variety of functions or roles.

Primary functions.   Although not represented on all campuses, four primary general university extension functions can be identified:

First, the direct transmission of regular university course study to people who, for whatever reason, cannot come to the campus but who seek academic credits. In carrying on this function, extension is under pressure from both internal and external sources to replicate as exactly as possible the pattern of residence instruction, so as to in no way jeopardize the applicability of credits earned toward an academic degree.

Second, the transmuting of regular university instruction into patterns tailored to meet the intellectual, cultural, or vocational needs of youths and adults. Originally this function was largely remedial in nature; that is, it brought fairly elementary learning to persons previously unexposed to much education. Increasingly, informal instruction has come to represent higher levels of content, appealing now largely to college graduates who seek periodic refresher experiences. Indeed, some extension instruction today is more sophisticated than any regular campus work.

Third, the placing of university departments and schools into a direct and essentially consultative relationship with secondary schools, libraries, state and federal agencies, organizations, groups, communities, industry, unions, counties—the gamut of public associations. This function inevitably sounds rather amorphous on paper, but in practice it can be an intensely meaningful one.

Fourth, the actual creation of new, substantive agencies within the university, sharply attuned to emerging public needs; and the creation or encouragement of new agencies outside the university, focused on public problems.

Supporting functions.   In order to carry out these four primary functions, general extension will inevitably engage in three supporting functions:

First, reconnaissance. Through a variety of devices, organized and

informal, extension serves as the eyes and ears of the campus, fer-
reting out public problems, deducing public needs, verbalizing
public aspirations, and transmitting these impulses back to the university, where they form the basis for new directions in research and
teaching.

Second, program development. Extension is not simply com-
pounded of response to demand. The utilitarian university is sensi-
tive to the felt needs of its constituency, but programming does not
wait passively upon requests for service.[4] As Van Hise put it long
ago: "We in education ought to be at least as vigorous as the brew-
ing interests. . . . It is our aim to take out knowledge whether the
people ask for it or not."[5] An acceptance of this philosophy leads
extension into a set of activities similar to, although more refined
than, what business would call product development and promotion.

Third, applied research. Before it has viable data to extend, extension must frequently find the facts. As residence departments
move increasingly into the orbit of basic research, extension divisions are assuming more and more of the applied-research function.

Devices

Asked to define the "instruments of extension," an early practi-
tioner said there were four: "correspondence teaching, lecture teaching, forum teaching, and bureau teaching."[6] This list is admirable in
its conciseness and may in fact represent all there is. But such a
distillation would hardly satisfy modern extensionists, with their long
rosters of extension devices. Pennsylvania State University, for example, has gone to great lengths to distinguish between institutes,
clinics, conferences, workshops, and several types of short courses.[7]
A compromise inventory of extension devices is that proposed by
Morton,[8] and it is his list that is used as an outline here, with the

---

[4] Richard J. Starr, "The Public Conscience of the University" (Chicago, 1955),
pp. 21–23. Mimeographed.

[5] *Proceedings* (Bangor, Maine: National Association of State Universities, 1908),
p. 131.

[6] William H. Lighty, *Report of the Dean of Extension Division* (Madison, Wis.:
The University of Wisconsin, 1918), p. 2.

[7] *Informal Adult Education Programs* (Berkeley, Calif.: The National University Extension Association, 1953), p. 8.

[8] John R. Morton, *University Extension in the United States* (Birmingham, Ala.:
University of Alabama Press, 1953), p. 131.

understanding that not all extension divisions maintain all these services, some may use still others, and some will prefer a variant nomenclature.

Correspondence teaching.   Antedating the formal establishment of university extension, teaching by correspondence was a tested method of adult education available for adoption as extension divisions were created university by university. Today, flanked by other instructional methods, correspondence teaching maintains a prominent—if no longer the preeminent—position in the array of devices utilized by institutions of higher learning in their outreach to the people.

Essentially, correspondence instruction is a method of guided self-study, a process of tutoring by mail. It involves the university in the preparation or selection of text books, syllabi, lesson assignments, and examinations. It involves the student in inescapable participation. The crucial factor in the quality of instruction carried on is the continuous exchange of correspondence between teacher and pupil. Correspondence instruction can penetrate the remotest corners of the state, and indeed, the nation and the world. No farther away than their mail boxes, it makes a reservoir of university resources available to the city dweller, the distant farmer, the prisoner, the invalid child, the shopkeeper, and countless others who wish to educate themselves as best their circumstances will allow. It does not depend upon the availability of special school facilities, nor does it require travel on the part of instructor or student.

Lecture services.   The "university list" of lecturers, the hallmark of early extension, is still in evidence. While the sustained educational value of the isolated platform performance has come into question, its utility for inspiration or stimulation cannot be denied. Common customers for such extension services are high school assembly periods, knife-and-fork clubs, conventions, and similar settings. The curriculum, if one can call it that, may include musical and dramatic performances, as well as speeches and scientific demonstrations. Performers are not necessarily members of the university staff. Frequently a series of lectures is presented as a many-sided approach to a particular topic. On occasion, also, the program format will provide for audience discussion, in which case the term "forum" may be used. A lecture series can even take the form of an overseas study tour.

Summer-school programs.   The summer school and extension share a common ancestry, and many of their outward characteristics remain similar. The summer campus is frequently the setting for a wide range of clinics and workshops serving the needs of youths and adults. In many institutions the dean of extension is also the director of the summer session. However, the summer school has evolved as really quite a different breed from extension. While continuing to offer noncredit programs, at heart the summer session is simply the continuation of the regular university enterprise throughout the summer. Increasingly its student body is made up of matriculated students taking regular courses. As universities seek to accommodate more and more undergraduate and graduate students, the trend toward various types of year-round calendars will no doubt accelerate, and summer sessions may well lose what remains of their outreach orientation.

Extension classes.   Stemming directly from the lecture hall and the classroom, the extension class represents the most elemental and traditional form of university teaching: face-to-face confrontation of professor and students. Extension classes may be highly formal, strictly following the syllabi of standard university courses and adhering to the same standards of perfection, examinations, and accomplishments; sometimes diplomas and certificates are issued as evidence of successful completion of such a course or sequences of courses. In other cases, the courses may be most informal, in no way requiring an exact campus pattern, tailored instead to fit the educational needs of a particular group or clientele as perceived by them and their instructor. In a land covered by classrooms or other suitable facilities—in public schools, public and private technical institutes, even factories, homes, taverns, and shopping centers, extension classes remain one of the most flexible devices employed by the university for making its resources available to people over a greater area than its home campus.

Press and publication services.   The printed word has always been a form of extension outreach. Through folders, bulletins, monographs, and even books, extension divisions transmit university facts and insights, both independently or in conjunction with other forms of extension teaching. Some titles are reports of esoteric research, aimed primarily at scholars in other climes. Others are popularized versions or compilations of university studies. Still

others are how-to-do-it manuals. On occasion an extension publication has become a "best seller." Most are distributed at cost or given
away. A special form of publication service is the extension magazine, typically a quarterly devoted to a particular area of activity.

Extension centers and evening schools.   In the process of organizing extension classes over a wide geographic area of the state, there
was bound to be some concentration of programs in those locations
providing the most suitable facilities and responsive clientele. This
concentration in turn was conducive to both repetitive and sequen-
tial programming, leading to the eventual institutionalization of university extension activities in various centers away from the campus.
As valuable facilities for equalizing educational opportunities, centers are now accepted as standard university agencies and are being
readied to assume increasing responsibilities appropriate to the
university.[9] Many serve as focuses for informal adult education and
community-service activities. In their collegiate program, extension
centers typically provide the first year of lower division work, usually
the second year as well, and less frequently, the entire sequence
leading to the bachelor's degree. Sometimes centers develop into
university branches and, as such, do not remain long under extension auspices. Some eventually become independent institutions.

The same forces, interests, and needs which produced extension
centers for the dispersal of university teaching over a wide geographic base led to the creation of evening colleges through which
greater numbers of people gain ready access to universities in or
near their home. Having so established their own identity or, con-
versely, in some cases, become so integral a part of their institutions,
evening colleges are now less frequently thought of as extension
agencies. Nonetheless a number of extension divisions still admin-
ister these facilities, as attested to by some overlapping membership
in the National University Extension Association and the Association of University Evening Colleges.

Sometimes referred to as evening divisions or evening schools,
these agencies differ widely with respect to practices, programs, and
administration. Two characteristics, however, are common. First,
they are based predominantly in municipal, private, or denomina-

---

    [9] Christian K. Arnold, "Community Campuses," *Saturday Review* (March 17,
1962), p. 37.

tional colleges and universities in relatively large cities. Second, they offer programs of instruction in the same city, ordinarily, in which the main institution is located, but, as their name indicates, in late afternoon and evening hours, making their curriculums more readily accessible to the general public.[10] Like extension centers, evening colleges are typically not innovators in their certificate and degree programs, but rather attempt to duplicate the day college program in every way possible. In their noncredit programs, however, evening colleges are much less encumbered by day-school requirements and in this realm often manifest great imagination and versatility.

Library materials lending services. In many extension divisions will be found a "bureau of information" which encompasses a variety of activities similar to those performed by a large and vigorous urban library. These may include: compiling and lending "package libraries" of printed materials on public questions; preparing study outlines on current topics; preparing bibliographies and briefs on debatable subjects; duplicating informational bulletins on specific questions; assisting interscholastic debating societies; assisting civic clubs, women's clubs, and similar organizations in program planning; supplying information on miscellaneous matters in response to spot requests; and organizing community forums. Some of these services are rendered directly to individuals and groups; often, however, the bureau functions as a wholesaler, back-stopping the resources of a small local library or school system.

Audio-visual aid services. Closely related to the library materials lending service is the extension bureau which collects, catalogs, evaluates, distributes, and even produces slides, film strips, tapes, motion pictures, records, displays, and other audio-visual materials. Schools and discussion groups are the primary customers. Frequently this bureau will support on-campus instruction, as well as integrate its activities with other extension operations.

Conferences, institutes, and short courses. The use of intensive short-period instruction has grown rapidly recently in extension divisions throughout the country. It suits the American temper, it meets the needs of professional people particularly, it gives immediately perceived results; it offers opportunity for collaboration in virtually every field of knowledge or human activity; and it is per-

---

[10] John F. Dyer, *Ivory Towers in the Marketplace* (Indianapolis: Bobbs-Merrill Company, Inc., 1956), pp. 27–29.

haps the most favorably regarded of extension activities by the residence faculty. A typical institute will see a group of 30 or 40 people of like mind or vocation assembled on the central campus for two or three days of lecture, discussion, and practical work on a topic of vital interest. It would take many pages of this book to list the groups participating in such instruction and the subjects that they deal with. The work is almost without exception non-credit; frequently it is interdisciplinary.

Broadcasting services. University extension sought to utilize radio almost from the inception of this medium. A number of universities now own and operate radio stations, some in alliance with state or regional educational networks. It was early discovered that, with some exceptions, existing extension devices and personnel could not be aired without considerable adaptation, so extension by radio has tended to develop its own specialists. In many cases their programming has been most imaginative. Where these personnel do not have campus stations, they develop taped programs for broadcasting over commercial outlets seeking "public service" credits. The decline of evening radio as an advertising medium has opened up a good deal of air time for extension-produced tapes. In general, these take the form of informal talks, panel shows, and group discussions, with some dramatic productions in evidence.

When television burst on the horizon of extension, it was initially considered the answer to long supplication, but its performance has not matched its promise. Some universities maintain television stations and others produce kinescopes, films, and videotapes for consumption by commercial stations, but the costs involved in either activity are prohibitive without public subsidy or student fees. What is more, the image of open-circuit television as an entertainment medium appears to be so strong that listeners find it difficult to watch educational broadcasts in a learning frame of mind. Extension keeps trying, however, to find the key to the use of television as a consistently efficient outreach device. Closed-circuit television is coming into increasing use in support of extension teaching in centralized facilities.

Special service activities. Under this heading Morton combines many kinds of informal instructional liaison with communities, institutions, and a wide variety of interest and professional groups.[11]

---

[11] Morton, *op. cit.*, p. 136.

Activities range from the most casual type of consultation with, for example, a businessman, to the providing of secretarial services for impecunious but worthy causes, to an elaborate community theater project, to a long-range study of regional resources. Frequently such services will be in the nature of buttressing the activities of other educational agencies. Typically the services will be carried out cooperatively with appropriate lay organizations. On occasion, however, extension may feel required to stimulate action in the absence of viable agencies, though when it does so it will simultaneously attempt to create an extra-university organization that can carry on the activity.

Articulated instructional media. The tendency of extension divisions to think of and organize themselves in terms of fairly discrete devices of outreach has lent considerable effectiveness to each of these instruments of instruction, but it has also had the unfortunate effect of introducing a good deal of rigidity into extension programming. Recently a number of efforts have gotten under way to combine or "articulate" the various media in ways that will optimize the resulting instruction. A typical student in such a program might take one course through a combination of correspondence instruction and group study; another through summer session, independent study, and field laboratory; a third by television and evening class; a fourth by tel-lecture, correspondence, and weekend conference; and so on.[12]

Physical Facilities

In the performance of their mission, extension divisions operate or use a variety of facilities. First, there must be an administrative headquarters on the central campus. It may be only a single office or suite of offices, or an entire building. Second, there may be an institute and conference building, frequently called a "continuation" or "adult education" center, again on the central campus. This facility may provide room-and-board accommodations as well as meeting rooms. Third, off-campus centers may have their own buildings; so may evening colleges, the latter often "downtown" in the heart of the city. Where extension does not have its own facilities, it makes

---

12 Charles A. Wedemeyer and Gayle B. Childs, *New Perspectives in University Correspondence Study* (Chicago: Center for the Study of Liberal Education for Adults, 1961).

arrangements for classroom and conference space wherever it can, hopefully but not necessarily in a building with an educational "image." Local schools, libraries, and auditoriums are used most frequently; but it is not unknown for an extension group to meet in the men's "lounge" of a factory, in a church basement, or even in a bowling alley. If extension has contributed anything to American understanding, it is that ivied halls are not an essential concommitant to learning. However these egregious surroundings have not made it any easier to assure many faculties that what goes on in them is worthy of a university.

Personnel

Because university general extension is not a fully recognized "career line," its practitioners represent a wide range of academic and professional backgrounds, and there is a comparatively high rate of attrition. There is a growing tendency to recruit Ph.D.'s, on the assumption that a devotion to scholarly research on the part of the extension staff helps to raise the stature of the extension division in the eyes of the university community. What this trend will mean in terms of practical outreach remains to be seen. Extension teachers typically come either from appropriate residence departments or from the respective professions. Extension administrators tend to have either extensive university or business backgrounds or both. Interestingly enough, most extension directors to date have been recruited from outside the discipline of education. Increasingly, however, young men trained in the theory and practice of adult education are appearing. They are generally eager and intelligent, but require considerable experience with the realities of program development.[13]

The success of any university extension operation depends in large measure on the capabilities and objectives of the personnel involved. The problem of staff recruitment, training, and motivation is discussed more fully in Chapter IV.

---

[13] Baldwin M. Woods and Helen V. Hammerberg, "University Extension Education in the United States," in *Universities in Adult Education* (Paris: UNESCO, 1952), p. 145.

Clientele

It is very difficult to generalize about university general extension students other than to say that substantial enrollments, representing a wide range of interests and vocations and ages, can be documented fairly accurately by any extension division. A number of studies, some of them well-conceived and controlled, are beginning to shed some light on the matter.[14] At the outset two general conclusions can be made: first, each method of extension, and each type of program within each method, tends to attract a homogeneous and unique clientele;[15] and second, each region of the country, and each institution, exhibit different clientele patterns.[16] Given these divisive tendencies, any further synthesis is admittedly risky. Houle offers this broad assessment:

> In general, high-income groups are more likely to take part . . . than low-income groups. Participation is also positively related to the size of the community. . . . People with certain nationality and religious backgrounds are more active than those with other backgrounds. Age is important: . . . there is a sharp upturn in the late twenties, a fairly constant level of activity until the age of fifty, and a decline afterward. Married people participate more than single people. . . . Many more professional, managerial, and technical people take part relative to their number in the population than do people from other occupational groups; next in significance are white-collar and clerical workers; then skilled workers; and lastly unskilled laborers. The most universally important factor is schooling. The higher the formal education of the adult, the more likely it is that he will take part in continuing education.[17]

The question of the comparability of adult students to college students in learning ability or scholastic aptitude has been empirically studied, and the consensus is that extension students are at least equivalent in mental abilities to their residential student counterparts.[18] Research into the scholastic achievement of adult students

---

[14] Coolie Verner and John S. Newberry, Jr., "The Nature of Adult Participation," *Adult Education* (Summer 1958), pp. 208–20.

[15] Harold Montross, "University Extension Students," *Adult Education* (Autumn 1959), p. 56.

[16] Morton, *op. cit.,* p. 71.

[17] Cyril O. Houle, *The Inquiring Mind* (Madison, Wis.: The University of Wisconsin Press, 1961), p. 7.

[18] A. A. Lacognata, "Adult Education Performance" (East Lansing, Mich.: Michigan State University, n.d.), p. 1. Mimeographed.

suggests evidence that adult students are at least equal to under-graduate students here as well.[19]

Why do adults continue their education? Houle postulates three groups: the goal-oriented, those with fairly clear-cut academic, economic, or professional objectives; the activity-oriented, those who take part because they find in the circumstances of the learning a meaning exclusive of the content; and the learning-oriented, those who seek knowledge for its own sake.[20] These are not pure types, of course; there are many mutations.

In summary it can be said that two basic facts seem to underlie university extension participation: (1) it is not a chance event in a person's life but is determined by his needs, and (2) he looks to education as an aid in realizing his aspirations. Extension education thus is rooted in the social situations in which adults find themselves.[21]

Curriculum

In keeping with extension's mission "to provide opportunities for individuals of all ages, of all economic levels, of all professions, . . . singly and in groups,"[22] university extension's curriculum becomes extremely broad, representing versions and conversions of almost every subject-matter area and research interest of the parent institution, and then some. Indeed, extension is frequently accused of spreading itself too thin. To lend some sense of focus and priority, extension leaders have recently proposed a number of "program areas of primary concern:"[23] (1) education for adults whose regular academic program has been interrupted, (2) technical, professional, and postgraduate education, (3) opportunity throughout life for intellectual growth and creative activity, (4) education for family living and the advancing years, (5) citizenship education for civic literacy and public responsibility, (6) education for international cooperation, (7) community development programs to cope with

---

[19] Roger De Crow, *Ability and Achievement of Extension Students* (Chicago: Center for the Study of Liberal Education for Adults, 1959).

[20] Houle, *op. cit.,* p. 16.

[21] Charles E. Chapman, "Some Characteristics of Adult Part-Time Students," *Adult Education* (Autumn 1959), p. 40.

[22] *Report of the Policy Statement Committee,* p. 6.

[23] *Ibid.*

the problems of urbanization. In assessing this curriculum, if one can call it that, it is well to remember that "when extension leaders discuss educational needs of adults and describe educational undertakings, they give the impression that their concepts and hopes are much nearer realization than the facts indicate."[24]

Assessments

As a University of Minnesota president mused somewhat plaintively, "How do you assess the results of a university?"[25] There are no exact butterfat standards or soil tests against which to measure the efficacy of university enterprise in general or extension in particular. The situation is complicated by the fact that the university and its general extension arm have tended to take all knowledge as their ordinate and all society as their abscissa. To the question of whether or not America has thereby been improved, some educators are apt simply to ask in return, "Would you be willing to go back to the '90's?"[26] Intriguing as is such a sweeping evaluation, it is hardly satisfactory.

Commentators and committees have been evaluating extension periodically for many years, and, not surprisingly, the report card grades have ranged from good to bad to indifferent. It is interesting if not significant that the muckrakers of yesterday were uniformly high in their praise of the new utilitarian university. Lincoln Steffens observed, for example, that "the university is using the conscious demand for 'utilitarian' instruction to develop the unconscious demand that exists in the American people today for light." He looked forward to the time when the university would "distribute scientific knowledge and the clear truth in plain terms to all people for their self-cultivation and daily use."[27] Many other observers thought they saw, beyond the extension courses in sanitary sewerage, highway construction, and shop mathematics, the promise of a new, completely informed, progressive America.

[24] Woods and Hammerberg, *op. cit.*, p. 128.
[25] James Lewis Morrill, *The On-Going State University* (Minneapolis: The University of Minnesota Press, 1960), p. 24.
[26] Cyril O. Houle, "The American University and Adult Education," *The Educational Record* (October 1955), p. 388.
[27] *American Magazine* (February 1909), p. 363.

Before such glowing tributes are dismissed as immature and premature, it is well to remember what many men of the time were honestly afraid of—a revolution on the part of the restless, unskilled masses of unemployed. William H. Lighty, admittedly an extension enthusiast, concluded that extension did indeed prevent the alienation of groups and classes. Even E. A. Birge, hardly an extension devotee, was willing to say that extension was an "indispensable instrument" in the building of a peaceful, prosperous American society. In retrospect, it is difficult to visualize extension as standing between the social fabric and revolution, but this is born of hindsight.[28] Certainly university general extension has helped bring education and training to millions in the past 60 years, and it would be difficult to prove that this has not in some way contributed to a vigorous yet stable society.

The measure of university extension may also be taken in part from a review of the instrumentalities that currently are taken for granted in American life but which trace their origins to university extension enterprise. It has always been extension's role to pioneer, to fill the gaps, and then to "work itself out of a job" by creating or encouraging substitute agencies. This role general extension has performed with an aplomb that is amazing in the light of the resistance an institution ordinarily exhibits to changing directions. Vocational schools, community colleges, branch campuses, professional organizations, lecture bureaus, traveling library services, public health associations, welfare departments, little theaters, municipal reference centers, discussion clubs, school standards agencies, debate societies, urban leagues—these and many other activities and organizations have been "mothered" over the years by university extension and then prodded out of the nest.

As extension has changed the alliances of society, so has it changed the campus. Institute and conference topics have become college courses and even entire degree sequences. Extension questions have led to substantial investigations and even to major research programs. Extension students have become active friends of the university and have contributed time and money to its support.

But extension-wrought changes have not been greeted with universal acclaim. In 1930 Dr. Abraham Flexner accused general ex-

---

[28] Frederick M. Rosentreter, *The Boundaries of the Campus* (Madison, Wis.: The University of Wisconsin Press, 1957), p. 81.

tension of robbing the university of the "unity of purpose" and "homogeneity of constitution" which he deemed the prerequisite of a true community of scholars. More recently a variety of commentators have accused extension of robbing the public of "liberalizing" attitudes through an over-emphasis on the commercial and the material. Gordon has even suggested that university "service" is best described by an archaic Websterian definition: "the attention and devotions of a gallant to his mistress."[29] The latter-day Flexners have been particularly critical of functional extension's "community development" bent. "The proper goal of adult education," says Benne, "is not to solve social or personal problems . . . but to infuse into (public and private) deliberations . . . something of the intellectual functions of the knowledge-seeker."[30] By contrast, Powell calls community development services "the *most* fully adult programs within the gamut of university extension."[31]

This persistent logomachy is characteristic of extension sounds and sights today. Certainly it is true that extension in time of national stress has "stood tall" as an instrument of America's survival. Yet it is equally true that the two states with the biggest university extension budgets have contributed to American political life the most notorious individuals and movements of recent times. While extensionists themselves like to think that extension divisions have rendered substantial educational contributions, they concede that great gaps continue to exist between their high ideals and actual performance, that general extension is still often a step-child of the university, and that public educational needs continue vastly to exceed the wherewithal and maybe even the wisdom of university extension.[32]

Working together, men of action who could appreciate the dreamer, and idealists who were not averse to action, have indeed

----

[29] Morton Gordon, "The Meaning of University Level," *Adult Education* (Autumn 1959), p. 23.

[30] Kenneth D. Benne, "Adult Education in the University," in *On Teaching Adults,* (ed.) Marilyn V. Miller (Chicago: Center for the Study of Liberal Education for Adults, 1960), p. 23.

[31] John Walker Powell, *Learning Comes of Age* (New York: Association Press, 1956), p. 86.

[32] Ralph W. Tyler, "An Evaluation of General Extension in Land-Grant Institutions," *Proceedings of the American Association of Land-Grant Colleges and State Universities,* Vol. II (Kansas City: The Association, 1961), 135–54.

broadened campus boundaries.[33] As these extensionists have moved out to come to grips with people's problems, the people in turn have brought to the American university the interest and support it has needed to become an educational institution of "outstanding achievement and influence." But the end is not yet. Only a minority of the population continues its education throughout life through organized programs. To attain the necessary goals will require on the part of all universities "new commitments, new directions, and more efficient employment of resources."[34]

Until a time is reached in the history of the world when there are enough mature, knowledgeable people in the right places at the right moments, there will be a job for adult education. Whether the record and the promises of university general extension justify continued investment in this particular institution is for today's extensionists to demonstrate.

---

[33] Rosentreter, *op. cit.*, p. 172.
[34] Tyler, *op. cit.*, p. 21.

CHAPTER III

Agricultural Extension

Agricultural extension is often described as the most effective adult education activity in the United States, one of the oldest, probably the largest, and certainly the most fully developed.[1] Yet a recent book on university adult education limits its discussion of agricultural extension to an appendix, with the explanation that agricultural extension has only an incidental relationship to the university and is an anachronism in modern America anyhow.[2] The ambivalence in attitudes toward university agricultural extension is understandable. Agricultural extension is a unique service, with its feet in farm soil and its head in a campus seminar. It involves three levels of government. It tries to reflect flexibility and adaptability to local conditions and needs while expressing a national sense of purpose and focus. And "ag" extension is attempting to operate today in a changing milieu that calls for dramatic adjustments on the part of servers and served.[3]

Agricultural Extension Today

As a generic term, university agricultural extension may include a wide range of service activities undertaken by a (typically land-grant) college or university for rural people. In practice, however, most such activities are channelled through the Cooperative Extension Service, and it is this specific organization that is discussed in this chapter. In essence, Cooperative Extension work in agriculture (and home economics) is a partnership undertaking between each state land-grant college and university and the United States Department of Agriculture, in cooperation with local governments and

---

[1] Everett M. Rogers, "How Research Can Improve Practice," *Theory into Practice* (April 1962), p. 89.

[2] Renee and William Petersen, *University Adult Education* (New York: Harper & Row, Publishers, 1960).

[3] *Scope Report* (Washington, D.C.: American Association of State Universities and Land-Grant Colleges, April, 1958), p. 3.

local people. The major function of the Cooperative Extension Service, as stated in amended federal legislation, is ". . . to aid in diffusing
among the people of the United States useful and practical information on subjects relating to agriculture and home economics, and
to encourage the application of the same . . ." This function is
clearly education, but not in the classical sense: it is informal education for action.

In performing its assigned mission, the Cooperative Extension
Service aims at "helping people to help themselves in attaining more
efficient farms, better homes, higher incomes, richer living, and increased competency in group action." In so doing "the CES takes
to rural people the results of research and practical experience, as
well as information with respect to pertinent government programs."
In recent years CES workers are said to have "taught" some four
million rural families, plus two million suburban families.[4] The
workhorse of the system is the county agent, there being an average
of slightly over three agents per agricultural county in the United
States.

Antecedents and Development

Agricultural extension work is sometimes thought of as having
been created by the federal Smith-Lever Act of 1914. It is true that
the Smith-Lever Act established the Cooperative Extension Service
per se, but the county agent had arrived on the scene earlier in the
form of federal, state, or local "agricultural representatives." The
Smith-Lever Act brought order out of overlapping activities and
introduced matching funds to assure formal collaboration.

Early impulses.[5]   As early as 1785, public-spirited people in
Pennsylvania, Massachusetts, South Carolina, and elsewhere imi-
tated the English and other Europeans by establishing agricultural
societies dedicated to the improvement of farming. The societies
urged the importance of breeding better animals and plants, they
encouraged the discovery of better methods of tillage, better tools,
and better machinery, and they urged that reports of such improvements and discoveries be communicated to the public. The societies
themselves published reports and encouraged the federal and state

---

[4] *Ibid.,* p. 4.
[5] Based on unpublished manuscripts by Vernon L. Carstensen, Professor of History, University of Washington.

governments to do likewise. By 1850, 20 of the 31 states then comprising the United States were taking a periodic census in which agricultural data formed a substantial part. In 1839 federal funds were provided for the commissioner of patents to collect and distribute agricultural statistics. Moreover, other devices were conceived to further the same goals. Agricultural fairs multiplied in the nineteenth century. Here men could exhibit the fruits of their husbandry and examine those of their neighbors. The appearance and growth of farm journals demonstrated another facet of the early preoccupation with dissemination of information.

Accompanying these various adult education movements for farmers was an agitation for education of youth in agricultural pursuits. All these developments and the aspirations they reflect were present in 1862 when Congress established the United States Department of Agriculture and passed the Morrill Act, which provided a land endowment to each of the states for the establishment of colleges of agriculture and mechanic arts. These land-grant colleges and universities had no immediate success in formal undergraduate instruction, but they early came to establish agricultural experiment stations for exploring and testing improved farm practices. The researchers in turn felt a compulsion to disseminate their discoveries, and some did so vigorously through field demonstrations.

Over a period of time the federal Department of Agriculture evolved as a kind of national university. It collected information of all kinds relating to farming. It assembled a large staff of scientists, including some of the most distinguished in the country, to conduct research in many fields of learning, and it sought to teach the farmers of the nation. It also came to serve as a kind of agent of the agricultural colleges in the federal government and before the Congress. Directly and in conjunction with the college experiment stations, it became one of the big publishers in the nation—one whose books, monographs, and bulletins reached more farmers oftener than the catalogs of the mail-order houses.

The year 1887 brought the adoption by Congress of the Hatch Act, which provided each state with a federal appropriation for the support of agricultural experiment stations. The Act was itself evidence of the fact that the stations, which had already been established in a number of states, had attracted strong support.

Equally important were two new developments that offered the colleges better means of reaching their farmer constituency. The first was the development of farmers institutes in which the college staff and farmer representatives held two- and three-day meetings to discuss practical farm problems. A second development was the establishment of short courses under which farm boys, including those who had not graduated from high school, were enrolled in college for two short winter terms and given agricultural instruction.

But these developments, useful and popular though they were, did not provide fully for communication between farmers and the college, did not make fully and freely available to all what the college could offer, and did not permit the farmers to ask the questions they most needed to have answered.

At this juncture, in the first decade of the twentieth century, university general extension provided a pattern with its field representatives, peripatetic professors, and other forms of informal off-campus consultation. Simultaneously, in several parts of the country, the farm demonstrator, precursor of the county agent, appeared—in Texas in 1906 in conjunction with the campaign Seaman Knapp was directing to control the boll weevil, in Pennsylvania in 1910 in the effort to bring about the reoccupation of abandoned farms, in New York in 1911 under the aegis of business interests, and in other states as well. Some of these agents were employed by the federal government, some with the foundation funds, some by banks and railroads, some by chambers of commerce, some by the counties, some by the land-grant colleges, some by farmer organizations.[6]

The Smith-Lever Act.   The various public and private pressures that had accumulated to form the county agent concept were shortly at work in the halls of Congress, petitioning for a bill that would expand agricultural extension work under federal support and at the same time eliminate duplication of effort. In a real sense the resulting Smith-Lever Act of 1914 was revolutionary for its time. It projected a federal department into a firm alliance with state institutions. It was the first of many measures to require financial participation by the states on a matching basis. It spelled out fairly explicitly how the federal funds were to be used. It gave Washington a direct pipeline to rural America. And it solidified what Wis-

[6] Alfred Charles True, *A History of Agricultural Extension Work in the United States,* United States Department of Agriculture Bulletin No. 15 (Washington, D.C.: U.S. Government Printing Office, 1928).

consin's Dean Harry L. Russell called the "three-legged stool" organization for colleges of agriculture—research, resident teaching, and state-wide extension work. The Act has been amended from time to time and its appropriations steadily increased, but the structure it established has remained remarkably unchanged for fifty years, modified only by occasional administrative memoranda of agreement between the land-grant colleges and the Department of Agriculture.

Growth. The Smith-Lever Act provided a way, as one farmer put it, "to bring science down out of the skies and hitch it to our plows." The states were prompt to respond with programs that would merit federal funds, and the ubiquitous county agent quickly became a hallmark of rural America. These men "peddled" progress. Some skeptical farmers classed them with lightning-rod salesmen, but along some road somewhere the agent would find the willing farmer who was to start America toward the astounding, prolific, scientific farm production we have today.[7]

Almost from the moment the Cooperative Extension Service was born, American agriculture began to experience a series of stresses that were to heighten the demand for CES programs. World War I, with its "feed the Allies" aspect, overtook the Service in its infancy. It responded with a yeoman emphasis on increased production. Fifteen years later it was administering the first of the depression measures designed to cut production. In another seven years the CES undertook to prove that a democracy could produce both guns *and* butter simultaneously. More recently the Service has been attempting to preside over a managerial reform in American agriculture that is bound up with mass shifts in land use, mass foreign aid programs, mass changes in the tools of technology, and the mass increases in educational levels—all in a political climate that continues to keep "the farm problem" a perennial football.

By 1965 there will be approximately 15,000 professionals on the CES roster in some 3,000 counties, and the total CES budget will be estimated at more than $150 million a year. This growth is in itself a tribute to the pioneer agents of fifty years ago. If the growth has been accompanied by a certain "hardening of the categories," it is only the inevitable concommitant of the institutionalization that

---

[7] *Fifty Years of Cooperative Extension in Wisconsin* (Madison, Wis.: Cooperative Extension Service, The University of Wisconsin Press, 1962), pp. 1–2.

has made the CES a stable servant of a rural America in the throes of explosive change.

Formal Organization

Although the Smith-Lever Act specifically provided for only two levels of cooperative extension organization, there was implicit in the movement the idea that local areas would be intimately involved, and the CES has therefore emerged as a triple-headed system. While its outlines vary somewhat from state to state, there is a strong thread of organizational uniformity.

Federal. Cooperative Extension Service workers are members of a Federal Extension Service and are eligible to participate in federal employee benefits. As such they report to the Secretary of Agriculture through the federal Administrator of Extension in Washington, who approves plans submitted by the states, injects some of his own, and releases federal appropriations. He has an administrative staff of some 60 supervisors and consultants.

State. At the state level there is a Cooperative Extension Service director allied with the land-grant college or university. Typically he is, or reports to, the dean of the college of agriculture. Under him are extension specialists in various subject matters, headquarters and district supervisory personnel, and field personnel in the counties. The state director formulates the broad program, coordinates extension workers, and administers the budget.

County. It is at the county level that the Cooperative Extension Service finds its focus. Here are agricultural agents, home-demonstration agents, 4-H club leaders, and other resident specialists. They report both to their state director and to a cooperating group within the county, which may be an informal group, a designated organization, or the county governing board. Lay individuals and groups furnish additional guidance and support. The county professional staff refines objectives and attempts to provide instruction that will lead to changed practices.

Informal Organization

If the Cooperative Extension Service depended only on its formal organization, it is doubtful if the system would work. In actuality the CES works in, through, and with a bewildering array of internal, created, and allied groups, organizations, and agencies that provide ways and means to affect farmer attitudes and farm practices.

Internal. As employees of the United States Department of Agriculture, Cooperative Extension Service workers have access to the resources of a large federal bureau. From time to time they have been asked to help implement various federal programs. Sometimes federal allegiance has projected CES people into political controversy, as in 1933 when they administered the Agricultural Adjustment Act. More often, federal assignments have brought heightened prestige and revenues, as under the War Food Administration in 1943. Recently federal programming has involved the CES in a lifting of sights under the Rural Area Development movement.

As faculty members of land-grant colleges and universities, Cooperative Extension Service workers have access to the teaching skills and research resources of their institutions. The institutions in turn have built a potent confederacy for the exchange of information and ideas and for representation in Washington.

As local employees, county agents can tap grass-roots cooperation in a manner and on a scale denied to outlanders. To professionalize their activities and career lines, CES workers have formed state and national fraternities.

Created. It is in the creation of "front" organizations that the Cooperative Extension Service has done some of its finest work. Looking in its early days for viable local vehicles of cooperation, the CES was instrumental in starting the farm bureaus that were to become the National Farm Bureau Federation. As a matter of fact, in some states agricultural extension and farm bureau activities were seemingly synonymous. As the Federation moved toward controversial political and economic positions, the CES sought to sever its ties, and in most states it no longer owes allegiance to a general-purpose organization.

The Cooperative Extension Service has helped form and maintain specialized organizations, however, to assist in furthering its educational work. With farmers there are dairy herd improvement associations, seed associations, poultry councils, artificial livestock breeding associations, potato spray rings, and so on. For farm wives there are homemakers' auxiliaries; for youth, 4-H clubs. With groups of farm families there are cooperatives of all kinds—for buying and selling and for the handling of farm and home supplies and farm produce. With agricultural businessmen, there are organizations of nurserymen, seedsmen, livestock breeders, farm equipment manufacturers, apple shippers, and so on.[8]

For the receipt of private funds the Cooperative Extension Service has created non-profit foundations. For interpreting CES needs to county boards, state legislatures, and the Congress, the CES has set up advisory committees. For handling testing and policing chores, it has helped build state departments of agriculture.

Allied. The Cooperative Extension Service does not exist in a vacuum. It must find its way through and with a persistent number of traditional community organizations and an ever-growing number of alphabet agencies.

The CES has built relationships with such local and state organizations as the church, the schools, community councils, PTA's, service clubs, chambers of commerce, planning boards, medical societies, bar associations, agricultural societies, fairs, women's clubs, Scouts, historical societies, resort associations, forestry groups, taxpayers' alliances, sportsmen, birdwatchers, and state agencies of all types, including its sister university general extension divisions.

Stemming from Washington are a staggering array of programs, with direct and indirect agricultural implications, with which the Cooperative Extension Service has made at least an uneasy peace. The CES handbook for one state lists the following such agencies—and expects CES workers to cooperate with them: FHA, ASCS, FS, REA, SCS, DA, DD, ES, ARA, SBA, HEW, HHFA, BR, GS, F&WS, IS, VA, PHS, RAD, OE, TVA, CD, DRD, CE, and DI.

Primary Programs and Processes

As has already been stated, Cooperative Extension is "fundamentally a means of teaching the people out of school about agriculture and country life in all its phases."[9] In going about this task, the CES has taken various approaches through the years.

---

8 Lincoln David Kelsey and Connor Chiles Hearne, *Cooperative Extension Work,* 3rd ed. (Ithaca, N.Y.: Comstock Publishing Associates, 1963), p. 96.

9 Edmund de S Brunner and E. Hsin Pao Yang, *Rural America and the Extension Service* (New York: Bureau of Publications, Teachers College, Columbia University, 1949), p. 6.

Traditional sub-divisions. At its inception, the Cooperative Extension Service was organized under three broad categories of work: agricultural extension, aimed at the farmer as a producer; home economics extension, aimed at the farmer's wife as a home-maker; and 4-H club work, aimed at farm boys and girls as future farmers and partners. In actual practice, these categories tended to phase into programs stemming from discrete academic departments on the campus or from sub-agencies in the Department of Agriculture. Thus the "curriculum," so to speak, of the county agent might include such manifold subjects or projects as dairy herd improvement, pea aphid control, rural zoning, field terracing, home canning, the school lunch, dressmaking, price supports, and so on.

Modern emphases. Although such topics still remain on the county dockets, in recent years there have been increasing attempts by federal and state Cooperative Extension Service leaders to think in terms of broad areas of major emphasis. Modern Cooperative Extension can be said to be geared to the following primary programs: (1) efficiency in agricultural production; (2) efficiency in marketing, distribution, and utilization; (3) conservation, development, and use of natural resources; (4) management on the farm and in the home; (5) family living; (6) youth development; (7) leadership development; (8) community improvement and resource development; and (9) public affairs.[10]

As can be seen, these primary programs cover the gamut of rural life. The topics are insightful and significant. But implementing such programs is difficult. They do not necessarily reflect the ways in which a university is organized, the ways in which federal programs are administered, or the ways in which people tend to view their problems. Despite these hazards, CES is imbued with a new sense of the "hard-core educational responsibilities" represented by these "areas of program emphasis."[11]

Procedures. How is a Cooperative Extension Service objective formulated, and how is it translated into a plan of work and thence into an action project in a farm community? The *Scope Report* of the CES implies a good deal of national and/or state direction to the field effort. On the other hand, the literature of Cooperative Extension is full of references to the claim that the role of federal and

---

[10] *Scope Report,* pp. 8–12.
[11] *Ibid.,* p. 14.

state leaders is simply to assist the counties in the accomplishment of programs propounded by country folks.[12] Probably the most realistic description of the actual procedure is that by Roger L. Laurence of Iowa State University, who says that extension programs can originate at the national, state, or county levels. Those that originate at the county level must gain state and federal approval before funds can be released. Those that originate at the federal level must gain state and local acceptance before they will be implemented. State-conceived programs likewise must gain topside approval and grass-roots acceptance. Understandably, then, uniformity in emphasis and methodology from state to state and county to county is difficult to attain, even if it were considered desirable.

In actual practice what seems to happen is that the county agent acts as a sort of "idea broker," interpreting federal and state aspirations and needs to his county council, and translating local needs and aspirations to his superiors. The net result is a reasonably "cooperative" enterprise, which finds its expression in lists of general and working objectives, primary programs, plans and calendars of work, and specific projects.

This seemingly tedious process of decision-making, with its lack of clear central direction, might appear to be calculated to produce either no action at all or multitudinous actions with no common chord. In actuality the unique Cooperative Extension Service structure and procedure has led to a self-sustaining organization, almost as political in nature as educational, with a remarkable independence from what it construes as extraneous pressures at any echelon, and with a dynamism of its own that has helped energize a peaceful economic and cultural revolution. Little wonder that the CES is looked on by some as a wonder of democracy and by others as an insidious "government within a government."[13]

Clientele

While the Smith-Lever Act referred generally to "the people of the United States" as the target for Cooperative Extension work, farm families were unquestionably envisaged as the major audience,

---

[12] Kelsey and Hearne, *op. cit.*, p. 195.
[13] Theodore Lowi, "How the Farmers Get What They Want," *The Reporter* (May 21, 1964), p. 34.

and the CES continues to affirm today that its "first responsibility is to farm families."[14] Increasingly, however, non-farm adults are showing up among CES clientele.[15] Included in this broader CES audience are non-farm rural residents; urban residents; farm, commodity, and related organizations; and individuals, firms, and organizations that purchase, process, and distribute farm produce, and that provide farm people with essential services and supplies such as credit, fertilizers, and feed.[16] Today, instead of concentrating on the problems of the farmer, the county agent, at least in a metropolitan area, "becomes a suburban family counselor on crabgrass, sprays for roses, and how to care for the new apple tree planted in the front yard."[17]

Exactly how many people the Cooperative Extension Service reaches is difficult to determine, because the CES reports participation on the total number of contacts, although one individual may have repeated contacts;[18] however, the actual number of people is undoubtedly large. Current CES documents put the figure at "over ten million annually." Of these, about two-fifths are said to be farmers, about one-fifth urbanites, and the balance various youths and representatives of agricultural business.[19]

The clientele of agricultural extension represents a wide spectrum in terms of education. On one hand there is evidence that some "commercial agriculture has grown past agricultural extension," with college-trained farmers and agricultural businessmen looking to the commercial research worker or specialist for advice.[20] On the other hand, the proportion of adult farm people who have had only eight or fewer years of schooling is about twice that of the rest of the population.[21] It is perhaps not surprising, therefore, that in

[14] Scope Report, p. 13.
[15] Coolie Verner and John S. Newberry, Jr., "The Nature of Adult Participation," Adult Education (Summer 1958), p. 214.
[16] J. Earl Coke, "The Evaluation of Agriculture in Land-Grant Institutions," Proceedings of the American Association of State Universities and Land-Grant Colleges, Vol. II (Kansas City: The Association, 1961), 13.
[17] John C. Derlin, "New Task Facing the County Agent," The New York Times (June 29, 1964), p. m29.
[18] Verner and Newberry, op. cit., p. 214.
[19] Scope Report, p. 4.
[20] Coke, op. cit., p. 16.
[21] Theodore W. Schultz, "Meeting the Test of Higher Education," Proceedings of the American Association of State Universities and Land-Grant Colleges, Vol. II (Kansas City: The Association, 1961), 54.

the acceptance of new ideas and practices, rural sociologists have been able to identify those farmers who are "innovators," those who are "early adoptors," and on down to those who rarely if ever accept change.[22]

Methods

Cooperative Extension uses a variety of instructional devices. They may be characterized as informal and repetitious—informal because CES workers see the conventional lecture as "giving too much information in an uninteresting way," repetitious because experience has shown that people are influenced to make changes in behavior in proportion to the number of different teaching methods with which they come in contact.[23]

The method sanctified by legislative prescription and long practice is the demonstration—of either method or result, an effort to teach new farm practices by showing evidence of success. Seaman Knapp found the way when he was sent into the South in the early 1900's to fight the boll weevil. Choosing a good farmer here and there, he showed him how to cultivate part of a field, gave him simple instructions, brought him selected seed, and made frequent visits afterward to see that the directions were carried out. The neighbors promptly took notice and the next season did the same things, with the same results: good crops, earlier crops, crops that resisted the weevil.

Today farm and home demonstration work may range from a simple single demonstration, such as spraying an apple orchard or pressure canning, to much more elaborate demonstrations, such as soil conservation projects extending over wide areas and long periods of time. The guided tour and the farm field day are variations of demonstration work.

Personal farm and home visits are basic agricultural extension methods. Letters and telephone calls are sometimes substituted. Agricultural extension from its inception has made heavy use of the press. County agent news releases and columns have found ready acceptance, particularly in country weeklies. In more recent

---

22 George M. Beal and Joe M. Bohlen, *The Diffusion Process,* Special Report No. 18 (Ames, Iowa: Iowa State College, March, 1957).
23 Kelsey and Hearne, *op. cit.,* p. 413.

years the Cooperative Extension Service has made use of radio and television broadcasts, either independently or in cooperation with station "farm editors" or commercial companies. The bulletin is another form of CES instruction. "How to" manuals on almost every conceivable subject are mailed to rural box holders under the franking privilege enjoyed by the Service. Meetings, conferences, programs, forums, roundtables, seminars, symposiums, panel discussions, workshops—such group methods of informal instruction are also used by CES workers.

Sources of information most used by farmers vary with the stage in the adoption process: mass media are important in attracting awareness and interest; friends and neighbors are first in importance in evaluation, trial, and adoption.[24]

Evaluating Performance

What can be said about the impact of 60 years of agricultural extension? What can be measured? The contributions of agricultural extension have not been limited to the area of efficient production. Cooperative extension workers are fond of saying their ultimate aim is the development of people, and indeed their programs can be said to have led to better men, women, and children, through the more abundant life that increased income can buy. But such advances are hard to quantify. If bigger and better crops have been only a means to an end, they at least can be measured. Suffice it to say that from the start the CES has operated on the assumption that America is a materialistic civilization in which "advancement" is tied closely to income and richness to riches.[25] It is no disservice, then, to use this same yardstick in evaluating CES impact.

The pros. Our farm population today totals just about the same as it did a hundred years ago. The farmers of 1863 fed a population of little more than 30 million people. Today America's farmers feed more than 180 million in this country alone—and well enough to make personal weight control a nation-wide concern. One hour of farm labor in 1960 produced four times as much food and fiber as

24 *Adopters of New Farm Ideas,* North Central Regional Extension Publication No. 13 (East Lansing, Mich.: Farm Foundation and Federal Extension Service Cooperating, 1961).

25 Edward Danforth Eddy, Jr., *Colleges for Our Land and Time* (New York: Harper & Row, Publishers, 1957), p. 176.

in 1920; crop production was 65 per cent higher per acre; output per breeding animal was 88 per cent greater. Each U.S. farm worker today produces food for himself, for twenty other Americans, and for three persons abroad, with a surplus left over. In 1940 this farm worker supplied himself and ten other people, plus less than one person overseas. As the efficiency of the farmer has grown in this country, manpower has flowed from the farms into the cities to provide the labor needed by an expanding industry.[26]

To attribute these strides in agricultural production exclusively to agricultural extension is, of course, unreasonable. Even prior to the inception of the Cooperative Extension Service, the federal government, land-grant universities, and industry had established a reservoir of basic and applied research which has continued through the years to yield a fabulous flow of new knowledge. Various measures employed by the federal government have given farmers a monetary incentive to adopt improved farm practices and to retire marginal acres. Two world wars, two peaks of prosperity, and various subsidies have created and sustained a high demand for farm products.

Even granting these complementary forces, however, there is little doubt that the professional agricultural extension worker has played "a significant role in hastening the changes" that have led to astonishing accomplishments of technology and skill.[27] And it is worth pointing out that "the technological massiveness and intensity of agricultural programs have, on balance, accomplished more for consumers than for farmers, and have contributed relatively more to general economic growth than to improving the income position of agriculture."[28]

In recent years cooperative extension has extended its programs and processes overseas. On land-grant university campuses representatives from less developed nations come frequently to learn Cooperative Extension Service principles and techniques. And around the world today the sun never sets on American "county

---

[26] "The 16 Revolutions," *U. S. News and World Report* (March 14, 1958), p. 56.
[27] Kelsey and Hearne, *op. cit.,* p. 10.
[28] Paul A. Miller, "The Agricultural Colleges of the United States: Paradoxical Servants of Change," *Proceedings of the American Association of State Universities and Land-Grant Colleges,* Vol. II (Kansas City: The Association, 1961), 37–38.

agents" at work. Through the Food and Agriculture Organization of the United Nations and through various State Department agencies, CES alumni are lending an international flavor to the Smith-Lever Act.

Nor has agricultural extension been a one-way street. As it has carried knowledge from campus to cornfield, so has it carried back questions—questions that have spurred far-ranging research. The list of resulting discoveries is monumental. In dollars and cents their value has probably more than repaid the entire amount spent through the years on all agricultural research and extension.

The questions originating in agricultural extension have not only stimulated research, they have led directly to the delineation of new teaching departments. Plant pathology, agronomy, agricultural bacteriology, dairy science, rural sociology—these and many other academic disciplines were unknown in the agricultural college of yesterday. The products of these departments in turn have contributed new dimensions to human understanding.

Cooperative extension has carried more than questions to the campus. It has carried public interest and support. The Cooperative Extension Service has been a potent factor in demonstrating to citizens and voters that the land-grant colleges and universities are not solely for the elite but for the mass of people as well. It is no accident that eight out of the ten American public universities that are considered outstanding teaching and research centers are universities with county agents.

The cons. But if agricultural extension is to share the credit for a production revolution, it must also share the blame for certain by-products.

Farm output is so large today that it is often depicted as a national disaster, rather than a triumph of man over his environment. Only by various artificial means is the country able to support farm prices, so distorted are the workings of agricultural supply and distribution. Even so, the benefits of this so-called farm progress are not being equally shared in rural America. Some 25 per cent of the nation's farmers produce 75 per cent of all farm products sold in the market. The remaining farms are grossly inadequate in terms of soil resources, capital goods, or management abilities. These marginal farmers survive at a level of living much below the national average. The human situations involved here are among the most difficult of the country's problems.[29] Agricultural extension has been remarkably unsuccessful in alleviating these pockets of rural poverty. Indeed, the CES has unintentionally yet surely widened the gap between the "early adopters" of improved farm practices and the subsistence farmers.

The human scars in the train of agricultural progress are matched by scars on the land: Dakota duck potholes drained to grow wheat, New York trout streams tapped to irrigate potatoes, Illinois fence-rows grubbed out to make room for more corn, Colorado hillsides grazed to the nub, Louisiana bayous reeking with the odor of spray-killed fish, Pennsylvania orchards silent in spring, Minnesota lakes silted by the detritus from eroded watersheds. Even when it has tried, agricultural extension has been unable to impart to most of its clientele a land ethic that represents a decent respect for the biotic community.

Perhaps it was too much to expect of agricultural extension that it stand between human and natural resources and the grinding advance of a technological avalanche. Perhaps it was never explicitly asked to do so. Certainly it has performed magnificently its duty as it has seen it—transmitting to American farmers the fruits of agricultural research. If the results of that transmission have sometimes been unfortunate, they stand as flaws in the American society that provides agricultural extension its orientation.

Extension's two-way street has not always carried blessings toward the campus, either. Practical questions have sometimes prompted an undue emphasis on "practical" research at the expense of the basic. The combined impact of Cooperative Extension Service money and energy has sometimes led to a skewing of university enterprise, with a college of agriculture flourishing in the presence of poverty-stricken liberal arts departments and a virtually nonexistent urban extension service.

In the final analysis, this distortion cannot be considered the fault of agricultural extension. It is, after all, the responsibility of university presidents and trustees to maintain a reasonably balanced institution.

A consensus.   The Cooperative Extension Service is, undoubt-

[29] Hans H. Landsberg, Leonard L. Fischman, and Joseph L. Fisher, *Resources in America's Future* (Baltimore, Md.: Johns Hopkins Press, 1963), p. 338.

edly, the largest single organized adult educational program in the world.[30] Woods and Hammerberg call it an "outstanding success" and "a model and example for other forms of adult education," one which has "partly closed the gap between research and application."[31] Burch agrees: "(The CES is) the outstanding adult education venture in the United States (which has) helped the farmer to upgrade himself economically and to work with others in improving the quality of home and family living."[32]

Miller says "there is no more massive, ponderous, and successful example of lasting connections with local groups and creating others. . . . It is doubtful that any other part of American life has recruited and commanded such an army of helpers who are able to reconcile their own need of personal and civic expression with the goals of a public agency."[33]

Now, more and more, agricultural extension "shares its once-held monopoly of technical competence with other agencies, public and private." Yet the local offices of the Cooperative Extension Service, facing partly toward the community and partly toward the university, form an indigenous institution in American life which is "perhaps the only arrangement in the United States capable of simultaneous local, state, and national education of either a formal or informal variety and which is so richly back-stopped by centers of permanent competence."[34]

Evaluating Future Needs

There are two broad ways to look at the continuing requirement for agricultural extension work. In both approaches figures can be used to prove diametrically opposite conclusions.

"CES is finished." In its early days, agricultural extension was operating in a country that was about two-thirds rural. Today the country is approximately two-thirds urban. The rural-farm population has dropped from 30 per cent of the nation, as late as 1920, to

[30] Verner and Newberry, *op. cit.,* p. 214.

[31] Baldwin M. Woods and Helen V. Hammerberg, "University Extension in the United States," in *Universities in Adult Education* (Paris: UNESCO, 1952), p. 132.

[32] Glen Burch, *Challenge to the University* (Chicago: Center for the Study of Liberal Education for Adults, 1961), p. 75.

[33] Miller, *op. cit.,* p. 26.

[34] *Ibid.,* p. 39.

7.5 per cent in 1960. The per cent of U.S. labor force engaged in agriculture has skidded in the same period from 26 per cent to 6.6. The country is losing farms at the rate of about 120,000 a year. The United States Department of Agriculture estimates there are now fewer than 3,000,000 *bona fide* farm operations in the country.[35]

These farmers are producing agricultural crops at a rate that piles up mountainous surpluses. In a seemingly frantic attempt to maintain the economy, the federal government on the one hand purchases and stores some agricultural surpluses and on the other pays farmers not to cultivate all their acres—in both cases, with tax monies. Yet American farmers even now are not producing as efficiently or effectively as they could, were they to apply all that is presently known about agricultural technology.[36]

Viewing from this perspective, some observers conclude that agricultural extension has worked itself out of a job. Is it not ridiculous, they say, that an increasing array of extension workers carries even more technological know-how to decreasing numbers of farmers who already produce more food and fiber than their fellow citizens can use, meanwhile draining the wetlands, grazing the woodlots, and usurping the fields that an industrial society needs for *lebensraum.*

According to this assessment, it would make more sense for agricultural extension to shift its programs to the suburbs and the cities, where modern people and problems cluster, and where the mechanisms of the Cooperative Extension Service could be directed toward helping find solutions to the vexations of the urbanite. Either that, or simply allow the program to atrophy.

"CES is just getting started."   Of the almost two million acres of land in the continental United States, no less than 90 per cent are devoted to farming, grazing, and forestry.[37] Although the number of farms has decreased, most of the land has stayed in production, as larger, more efficient farm operators continue to expand. This can be said to be the great geographic domain of agricultural extension. When the key raw materials of the American economy are grouped by origin and ranked by order of value, agriculture has

---

[35] Calvin L. Beale and Donald J. Bogue, *Recent Population Trends in the United States,* Agricultural Economic Report No. 23 (Washington, D.C.: United States Department of Agriculture, 1963), p. 46.

[36] Landsberg, *et al., op. cit.,* p. 340.

[37] Marvin, Clawson, *et al., Land for the Future* (Baltimore, Md.: Johns Hopkins Press, 1960), p. 442.

a clear first place.[38] Food is by far the largest single item in the American family budget, taking somewhat over one-fifth of all consumer expenditures, after taxes.[39] This is the great economic domain of agricultural extension.

At the beginning of the 1960's, the 180 million people of the United States enjoyed a higher level of living unprecedented in either their own country or any other. By the year 2000 the United States probably will have well over 300 million people who will want and expect even higher levels of living—better diets, better housing, more consumer goods of all kinds, better education and cultural opportunities, more facilities for recreation, and so on. Can the United States over the remaining years of the twentieth century count on enough agricultural production to provide the basis for a rising standard of living in the face of continued demands for defense, for the exploration of outer space, for assistance to less developed countries overseas, and for more land for urban uses?

This is the question faced recently by Resources for the Future, Inc., a nonprofit research center supported by the Ford Foundation. At the risk of oversimplifying the conclusions of the Corporation, it can be said that "continuing progress in (agricultural) technology and spread of skills and knowledge are the *sine qua non* of a continuing high standard of living based on an ample food supply available at a reasonable percentage of personal income."[40]

Using this point of departure, some observers conclude that agricultural extension is just getting started. If it is to contribute to meeting the food and fiber needs of America in 2000 A.D., they say, agricultural extension must hew to its traditional line—relocating producing areas, introducing new crop varieties, promoting the use of fertilizer, attacking the ravages of insects, diseases, and weeds, improving machinery, conserving the soil, and on down the list of production practices.

According to this assessment, for agricultural extension to flirt with so-called "total" area redevelopment programs or even with suburban lawn problems is a miscarriage of mission and public funds. Better that sister agencies be formed to accomplish for the city dweller what agricultural extension has sought to do for farm-

---

[38] Landsberg, *et al.*, *op. cit.*, p. 234.
[39] *Ibid.*, p. 89.
[40] *Ibid.*, p. 376.

ers, leaving the Cooperative Extension Service to concentrate on what it knows best, what it is best set up to accomplish, and what most needs doing—maintaining the viability of American agricultural production.

The upshot.   Which of these two views is correct? It is difficult to argue with the basic conclusions of Resources for the Future. If their premises are accepted, agricultural extension must be accorded an essential role in the next 40 years in bringing about the continuing and substantial improvements in crop yields required to feed a growing population. It does not necessarily follow, however, that agricultural extension can view itself as simply "more of the same." For one thing, its clientele is qualitatively as well as quantitatively different. The surviving agricultural entrepreneur is at least as sophisticated as the run-of-the-mill county agent, and his problems are more akin to those of a businessman than to those of a traditional dirt farmer. For another, the industries dependent on and supportive of agriculture are entering the field with independent research and educational programs. Finally, it is reasonable to assume that the efficiency and effectiveness of agricultural extension will itself increase as more is learned about interpersonal communications.[41] It took nearly 15 years for hybrid corn to move from university test plots to mass acreage. Today the lag between discovery and application is frequently no more than a year or two; farmers "buy any new product if someone will show them how it will cost out to their advantage."[42] These and other changes call for an "agonizing reappraisal" of the nature and scope of university extension services to rural America.

Indeed, it is no longer valid to draw a sharp distinction between "urban" and "rural" America, and hence between the agencies that serve the two regions. Farm and farmer stereotypes are passé. So are city images. A rapidly advancing homogenization of the American people, and a radical growth in suburbanization, are erasing most of the clear differences between country and metropolis.[43] Census takers can no longer clearly identify the geographic dividing lines. What distinctions remain will become hazier. The farmer is no more a man set apart in a rural class. City folks are moving to

41 Rogers, *op. cit.,* p. 93.
42 Victor Wartman, "The Farm Market," *Printers' Ink* (May 1, 1964), p. 28.
43 Landsberg, *et al., op. cit.,* p. 74.

houses on large lots which form strip cities along the highways. Urban infringement on farming is wryly illustrated by the incident of the farmer whose cows were dying from consuming golf balls.[44] Farmers and suburbanites alike commute to factories that are out in the open country under sky and clouds, surrounded by grass and parking lots. Both shop at the same composite centers which are re-creations of Main Street on the fringes of the cities.[45] Both share common sewer, water, school, and road problems. Each relies on the other in the operation of the American economy. As legislatures are redistricted, even politics will lose some of its traditional schisms. City and country are now tied together with a myriad of overlapping memberships and communications. An annexation of understandings has followed the annexation of territories. Community problems have moved from the private realm of decision in family, church, and store, to the public realm of government, the planning commission, and new forms of regional agreements. The growing interest of farm organizations in the broad philosophies of government rather than in the pursuit of limited and precise goals seems to preclude the lively concern they once had for the parochial needs of agricultural extension.[46] In this new America of "rurban" belts, adult education agencies will either reflect changing configurations, interrelated problems, and new needs, or they will become extinct.

Many decades ago Ezra Cornell commented on the opening of his university that there is "not a single thing finished." This would seem an apt motto for the land-grant institutions in their agricultural extension enterprise today. Coke urges the retention of the "strongest possible" agricultural extension program, and asks that agricultural extension not dilute itself by trying to "cover the waterfront." He rejects personalized agricultural extension to the nonagricultural population. Rather, he calls for a consolidation with general extension to provide a single off-campus educational service to an urbanized America.[47]

---

[44] Edward Higbee, *Farms and Farmers in an Urban Age* (New York: Twentieth Century Fund, 1963), p. 120.

[45] Dave O. Thompson, Jr., *Fifty Years of Cooperative Extension in Indiana* (Bloomington: Cooperative Extension Service, Indiana University, 1962), pp. 11–12.

[46] Miller, *op. cit.*, pp. 30, 33.

[47] Coke, *op. cit.*

"We cannot without peril overlook such a uniquely American innovation as the extension service to facilitate . . . continuing education throughout life on issues that count, as Miller says, but agricultural extension must achieve new forms of organization and administration at every level, must recruit and prepare persons of more varied backgrounds and potential than are now extant, and, in concert with general extension, must be brought to represent the entire university."[48]

The Cooperative Extension Service is a magnificent instrument for informal education for action. It is buttressed by generous public funds, an imposing organization reaching from Washington to every county seat, a unique combination of top-level program planning and grass-roots involvement, and a dynamism of its own that is constantly uncovering new areas of service. Yet this instrument represents only a small segment of the university and reaches only a small segment of society. In one case, "the principal university of a major manufacturing state spends more each year on 4H clubs than it does for its entire program of research and teaching for literally millions of industrial workers and their organizations."[49] The time is seemingly at hand for agricultural extension to lend its considerable skills and resources to the fashioning of a truly university-wide, community-wide outreach enterprise.

---

[48] Miller, *op. cit.,* p. 40.
[49] Frederic Heimberger, "The State Universities," in "The Contemporary University: U.S.A.," *Daedalus* (Fall 1964), p. 1092.

CHAPTER IV

Processes and Problems

From any survey of university extension, several broad impressions emerge: first, the university extension concept has the potential to rank as a major American contribution to human society; second, university extension in practice is distinguished by great variety; third, nowhere in any way has extension performance wholly fulfilled its promise; and fourth, present extension enterprise is no match for an age in which, to use Arthur Schlesinger's words, "science and technology have made the velocity of history so much greater than ever before."

Critical Factors

What are the problems faced by both general and agricultural extension today? Or, put another way, what are the ingredients of an effective university extension process? *There are at least ten critical factors:*

1. A clear-cut statement of the university's extension mission, incorporating dimensions, methods, priorities, and standards.
2. A sense of the significance of this mission and an ungrudging commitment to it on the part of the entire university faculty, from the chief administrative office to each individual professor.
3. A direct, consistent two-way channel between extension personnel and all the appropriate departments, schools, and colleges of the university.
4. A symbiotic relationship between university research and university extension.
5. Imaginative, coordinated extension administration.
6. An extension staff that merits and wins full fellowship in the university community while performing its essential mission.
7. An extension curriculum that reflects responsibility for institutional ideals and responsiveness to modern adult needs.
8. Effective teaching techniques and learning materials.
9. Adequate financing based on broad public support.
10. Viable communication to and from, and working relationship with, individual students, clientele groups, and sister agencies.

These critical factors represent a synthesis of those assessments begun by the United States Office of Education in 1930[1] and carried on by Creese,[2] Woods,[3] Morton,[4] Houle,[5] Tyler,[6] the Petersens,[7] Burch,[8] and others, including the authors.[9] The ten factors are obviously not co-equal. Some are wider in scope and more profound than others. Some are in a sense superficial; others are so complex as to defy ready analysis. Many are interlocking. In its total as a working outline, however, this summary of critical factors offers a relatively reliable guide against which all those concerned with the posture of American higher education can check the way in which a particular institution faces its third function.

There will be no single approach to any of the factors involved, because there is no single American university pattern. Indeed, one could say an approach indigenous to the campus and community concerned is a factor essential to any successful extension operation. But the considerations that must be faced in arriving at such an approach are remarkably similar from campus to campus.

Mission

What is the university's extension mission? What *ought* the university to do in the realm of public service? What *can* it do? On these questions there is confusion of counsel, and only the most

---

[1] *Extension Service,* Survey of Land-Grant Colleges and Universities (Washington, D.C.: United States Office of Education, 1930).

[2] James Creese, *The Extension of University Teaching* (New York: American Association for Adult Education, 1941).

[3] Baldwin M. Woods and Helen V. Hammerberg, "University Extension in the United States," *Universities in Adult Education* (Paris: UNESCO, 1952).

[4] John R. Morton, *University Extension in the United States* (Birmingham, Ala.: University of Alabama Press, 1953).

[5] Cyril O. Houle, *Major Trends in Higher Adult Education* (Chicago: Center for the Study of Liberal Education for Adults, 1959).

[6] Ralph W. Tyler, "An Evaluation of General Extension in Land-Grant Institutions," *Proceedings of the American Association of State Universities and Land-Grant Colleges,* Vol. II (Kansas City: The Association, 1961), 135–54.

[7] Renee and William Petersen, *University Adult Education* (New York: Harper & Row, Publishers, 1960).

[8] Glen Burch, *Challenge to the University* (Chicago: Center for the Study of Liberal Education for Adults, 1961).

[9] Clarence A. Schoenfeld, *The University and Its Publics* (New York: Harper & Row, Publishers, 1954); and Theodore J. Shannon, "A Study of Objectives for Selected Areas of University Extension," unpublished Ph.D. thesis, Yale University, June, 1958.

uncritical campus minds are free from doubt. In the first shy days of extension, some universities adopted the extension function freely and vigorously and cloaked it with what was for its time a well-formulated rationale. Other universities have "backed into" extension or have even assumed the function under duress. Faced with mountainous teaching and research tasks, all universities are now reconsidering their extension role, and "the responsibility of the university for adult education" has become a favorite topic for convention oratory. Presidents, laymen, and extension leaders agree that a clear statement of a university's extension mission is the necessary prelude to any consideration of other factors essential to extension success.

Alternatives. Suggestions are numerous. On the one hand there is the call for "total involvement with the whole of society's needs and aspirations . . . to provide opportunities for individuals of all ages, of all economic levels, of all professions, to benefit singly and in groups from the resources of (the university)."[10] On the other hand there is the counsel to "get back to the fundamentals . . . to insist on university standards and people of university caliber as students, . . . to be content with less far-reaching activities and build programs (in the conventional image of) departmental or college activities."[11] The fact that both of these statements stem from representatives of the University of California illustrates all too well the difficulty in arriving at an extension mission universally acceptable.

Most universities have little trouble accepting the geographic or chronological extension of credit courses as an appropriate and pertinent outgrowth of the essential purpose of a university—to discover and disseminate knowledge. In many urban universities today there are more part-time adult students than full-time, college-age students. Many state universities are rapidly decentralizing their campuses. Some faculties still accuse their extension colleagues of "soft pedagogy," and try to limit the number of extension credits that may be applied toward a degree; but other universities have so assimilated the theory and practice of conventional extension that

---

[10] *Report of the Policy Statement Committee* (Washington, D.C.: National University Extension Association, 1961), p. 6.

[11] Samuel B. Gould, quoted in *Federal Assistance to General University Extension Education Programs* (Washington, D.C.: Senate Committee on Labor and Public Welfare, 1962), p. 96.

they have assigned its supervision to the appropriate residence colleges rather than to the extension division.

A second type of extension—noncredit continuing education—is still eschewed in the more esoteric academic circles, but the parvenues of adult education consider it to be *the* most acceptable form. Indeed, some do not consider any credit courses to be *bona fide* adult education, even though adults are involved. Other adult educators, by contrast, are bent on building custom degree programs for adults, complete with special credits and diplomas. Campus traditionalists view this assault on the credit "gold standard" with all the horror another generation displayed toward William Jennings Bryan.

A related debate in continuing education centers around the perennial question of liberal versus vocational education. Continuing education has had perhaps its greatest growth in the area of professional and technical institutes and conferences, but a hardy crew assembled by the Center for Liberal Education for Adults has advocated programs that would emphasize the humane disciplines exclusively, or at least inject Plato or the Pleiades into discussions of automatic data processing.

It is about functional extension that some universities have the most qualms. The American university, say certain classicists, has gone too far with an overgrowth of "side" services. Others see functional extension turning the campus into a nonintellectual drugstore and quasi-academic repair shop. They view with abhorrence what Veblen called the "edification of the unlearned," and they wince at the implication that the university is merely responding subserviently to the demands of assorted "customers." Still others say that even if the concept of the utilitarian university were once valid it no longer is, in the presence of manifold private and public agencies designed to do what Van Hise and Harper set out to accomplish.

All such charges contain elements of truth. They lack, however, the recognition that enlightened functional extension is not simply a response mechanism. Functional extension will take into consideration educational, social, and civic standards as well as the needs of immediate concern to individuals and organizations; it will initiate as well as reflect urgent and important programs. In the final analysis, the argument about what constitutes "university level" extension work is as pointless as the medieval debate about how many angels could dance on the head of a pin. There are, fortunately, all sorts of colleges and universities with diverse configurations and missions. Any caveat on "university level" is a contradiction in terms. It is the *quality* of the *relationship* between campus and clientele that is the critical factor, not the type of student or form of outreach. This is not to say that an institution should not have standards for its extension work. The most precious of all university possessions is self-respect. When an extension division blurs the distinction between what is innately "right" and what is manifestly below par, the voice of the institution loses its note of clear conviction. But it is for each university to say what is "right" for itself. Certainly it is not demeaning for university experts to identify immediate public problems and to focus all existing institutional resources on a solution of those problems, or to create custom-tailored educational programs, in concert with appropriate professional and lay agencies.

Priorities. Each university cannot be expected to deal with all of the societal problems that come into its ken. The resources of individual institutions are rarely adequate for their tasks. A selection of priorities is therefore inescapable in any statement of extension mission. Lists will vary greatly from campus to campus.

A statement of the extension mission, then, must make clear what the university means by adult education and public service to the faculty, to participating citizens, and to the community as a whole. The statement should "reflect decisions as to the distribution of responsibility for clientele, areas, and levels of action-education among available agencies, with determination of those sectors in which the university will assume leadership."[12]

The university administrator, in short, must look carefully to his definitions. What in educational television, for instance, is learning and what is entertainment? Because these qualities rarely occur in a pure state, at what point does he bestow the stamp of approval? It is in such decisions that a university reveals its concept of extension.[13]

---

[12] Woods and Hammerberg, *op. cit.*, p. 131.
[13] Walter Argow, "Higher Education Para-Campus," *Overview* (June 1961), p. 39.

Commitment

For a university to adopt a coherent statement of its extension mission is not enough. The philosophy must be implemented. Implementation begins with an informed interest on the part of the president and constant contact between him and his extension chiefs. Implementation flowers in the presence of a commitment to the philosophy of university extension on the part of the entire university faculty.

The ideal. The extension ideal has in many ways best been attained by the land-grant college of agriculture. The college engages in resident teaching, in basic and applied research, and in widespread extension activities—all three activities frequently involving the same personnel and all three focusing on uncovering farm problems, investigating them, and transmitting new-found knowledge back to the farm and its environs. A general university extension commitment implies that the entire university be placed in the same relationship with all the people of a state or region as that achieved by the agricultural college with farmers. Implicit in such a commitment are two key requirements: the first, internal, that interrelationships among teaching, research, and outreach tasks and personnel come to pervade the entire campus texture; and the second, external, that effective relationships be achieved between all parts of the university and appropriate groups in society.

Two bonuses accrue from such a commitment: first, that a great deal of "unbudgeted" extension work gets done by teaching and research personnel in addition to their other duties; and second, that personnel who are assigned primarily to extension work attain full status in the university. Public service, in short, becomes *integral* rather than *peripheral,* to use Burch's words.

Some hurdles. The extension function is literally a logical extension of the university's age-old configuration of a community of scholars making itself as useful as possible. Extension can also be called a "public relations device." And from that springs one of the difficulties in the complete acceptance of the extension function by some people, on and off the campus. These critics insist on questioning the institution's motives. Houle, for example, calls extension's public-relations value its "greatest single handicap."[14] The fact is, however, that a university *must* maintain contact with all

---

[14] Houle, *op. cit.,* p. 42.

segments of the population—to keep open the doors to research and free inquiry, to obtain support from the constituency that sustains it, and to continue its acceptance as the highest order of a free institution of learning.[15] Thus it is advantageous that extension is a public relations device in the best sense of the term.

Another hurdle in the acceptance of the extension function is the fact that extension is deeply involved in the ordering of public values and public goals, and some people like to say such a role is either too controversial or too nonacademic to handle. This attitude is not unknown within extension units themselves. Instead of offering to reshape society, some extensionists have settled for studying it. Once they were firebrands. Now they are contemplatives,[16] eschewing any concern for the political or ideological environment. It is on unexamined concepts that these experts literally depend for their professional lives.[17] Yet the university as a whole, as a seeker and dispenser of truths, is inevitably concerned with values, if for no other reason than that values are themselves significant and moving facts. Extensionists particularly must not only be students of the values and goals of society, but they also must face squarely a sense of responsibility regarding the probable effects of their research and teaching on those values and goals.[18] Indeed, the long-term value of an extension staff is likely to rest quite heavily upon its ability to recognize and analyze the societal implications of its topical studies and instruction.[19]

Finally, operating against the assimilation of the extension function on the part of the university is the concept that adult education will always be, at best, a marginal university activity, and that adult education can therefore not come into its own until it emerges as a discrete discipline with its own separate institutions.[20] That there is

---

[15] *National University Extension Association Policy Report,* p. 8.

[16] Joseph Roddy, "What Is a Liberal?" *Look* (July 28, 1964).

[17] William J. Newman, *Liberalism and the Retreat from Politics* (New York: George Braziller, Inc., 1964).

[18] John E. Bebout, "The Idea of the Urban Extension Service" (New Brunswick, N.J.: Rutgers–The State University, January, 1963), p. 35. Mimeograph.

[19] Edward Schten, "Administration and Legislative Research," *Public Administration Review* (June 1963), p. 86.

[20] See Howard Y. McClusky, "Some Reflections on the Future of Adult Education," *First Annual Report of the Adult Education Association of the U.S.A.* (New York: The Association, 1952), p. 20; John Walker Powell, *Learning Comes of Age* (New York: Association Press, 1956), p. 162; and Coolie Verner and Alan Booth, *Adult Education* (New York: The Center for Applied Research in Education, 1964), p. 111.

need for reassessment, for coordination, and for cooperation in the vineyards of adult education, there can be no doubt. But it is not likely that total amalgamation will or should come to pass. A monolithic adult education organization does not reflect the way people live and the way institutions work. Each educational institution has its own self-selecting clientele. Each institution must cultivate its own constituency, in keeping with its central functions. Each institution needs in its own way the feedback that comes from a "walk in the ways of man." To say that a university can divest itself of its adult education responsibilities is only to say that a faculty wants to retreat to that status of a closed society which continental colleges prized and from which democratic universities have all too painfully escaped.

Old wine. Perhaps to attain a pervasive commitment to extension today there must come a recapturing of that initial impetus that sees the social role of the university as transcending its devotion to any one function or method or group, and a recognition of the fact that the university has become an irreplaceable instrument of national policy.

University extension was, in a real sense, a crusade, founded on high purpose, with the banner of inevitable human progress its colors. To quote one of its early supporters:

> The most important thing to say about university extension is that it should be directed and infused by Idealism. We may think of our Idealism as Moral Idealism, or Civic Idealism, or Social Idealism. It seeks out what is highest and best for humanity, it aspires to the finer achievements of life, it views material things and vocational pursuits as useful in proportion as they serve to promote the virtues of character and the deeds of goodness. The goal of our highest thought and effort in university extension will be to work toward that perfected humanity in which the well-being of each individual in organic relation with all others will be achieved.[21]

The words are out of style, but today as yesterday they are good words; they "blow into new heat the fires of idealism that tend to get smothered by the clinkers of failure, the ashes of success, and the non-combustibles of administrative activities."[22]

---

[21] Clyde W. Votaw in *Proceedings,* First National University Extension Conference (Madison, Wis., 1915), p. 316.

[22] R. J. Blakely, *Early Prophets in University Extension* (Iowa City: State University of Iowa, 1961), p. i.

Internal Relations

To be worthy of the name *university* extension, an outreach op-eration must be *of* and not simply *in* the university. By whatever means it is achieved, there must be a direct and consistent relation-ship between extension personnel and all offices, departments, schools, and colleges of the university. Some universities designate extension directors for each appropriate unit and leave them an-chored in their home departments, surrounded by their residence colleagues. Other universities pool these representatives in a central extension complex, but with lines of communication running back to residence units.

Carey identifies a definite life cycle, as he calls it, in evening col-leges and extension departments. According to him there are four stages of structural development: first, departmental domination, when extension is primarily the activity of campus departments, with no independent unit for adult education established; second, auton-omous development, when an identifiable or separate unit exists and major emphasis is placed on differentiating this unit from regular campus operations; third, integration, when the adult education unit comes to be accepted as an equal member of the university family; and fourth, assimilation, when extension activities, although per-haps still separately administered, come to be considered as integral and essential functions of the university.[23]

This pattern of growth does not take place in every institution, Liveright points out, and he suggests there is no ideal stage, that different approaches may be appropriate for different institutions. He believes, however, that in general it seems that extension pro-grams exhibiting the greatest degree of imagination, innovation, and experimentation are those in the third and fourth stages of growth, partly because those units in the second, autonomous, stage are "ex-pendable and insecure."[24]

Many would debate this conclusion. The form seems less crucial than the spirit, that spirit being to achieve close articulation of ex-tension programs with resident skills, and to build an understanding

---

[23] James Carey, quoted in A. A. Liveright, *Adult Education in Colleges and Universities* (Chicago: Center for the Study of Liberal Education for Adults, 1960), p. 9.
[24] Liveright, *op. cit.,* p. 9.

of the mutual interdependence of teaching, research, and outreach. In the absence of such an ethos, resident organizations do not accept extension ideas and extension personnel into full fellowship, and extension organizations do not utilize available resources fully or effectively. Agricultural extension has a particular problem. What Miller calls the "classic bureaucratic efficiency" of agricultural extension leads to an uneasy berth within institutions of higher learning "where there may exist the more genteel tradition that there should be no final administrative control over anything."[25]

Whatever the pattern of internal relations, it must be kept flexible, for there is emerging what John W. Hastie calls "a new revolution" in university organization and policies, characterized by a lengthening span of time devoted to particular investigations, by the establishment of new and novel research centers, and by changing relationships among fields of knowledge. With the growth of new studies that involve knowledge and practice of more than one of the traditional disciplines, and with the demand of students and government for research programs in complex subject-matter involving expensive and rapidly changing techniques and facilities, the university has responded with the creation of new departments, with interdepartmental—sometimes inter-university—endeavors, with research centers focused on particular areas of concern, and with new, elaborate equipment.[26] The fences between colleges and disciplines, in short, keep falling down. The agricultural colleges, for example, are no longer the single intellectual bastions they once were for generating new insights about the husbandry of plants and animals; the agricultural colleges in turn are sources of profound thoughts about human ecology.[27]

In the face of such changes, an extension organization must be prepared constantly to develop and maintain new, direct, and clear lines of internal communications. Indeed, the impulse for much of Hastie's "revolution" in campus organization should come from interdisciplinary extension reconnaissance.

---

25 Paul A. Miller, "The Agricultural Colleges of the United States: Paradoxical Servants of Change," *Proceedings of the American Association of State Universities and Land-Grant Colleges,* Vol. II (Kansas City: The Association, 1961), 26.

26 John W. Hastie, *Research at Cornell, 1961–1962: Annual Report of the Coordinator of Research* (Ithaca, N.Y.: Cornell University, 1962).

27 Miller, *op. cit.,* p. 30.

With new and old departments alike, extension's internal relations with respect to teaching will probably be governed by such ground rules as the following: If the curriculum to be offered is part of a degree sequence, the residence school will dictate the component courses and necessary student credentials. If the course to be presented is a credit course, the residence department will select (or at least approve) the instructor, prescribe or approve the course outline and the text, state any student prerequisites, and monitor the examinations. In the case of noncredit courses, on the other hand, the primary responsibility passes to extension. In some institutions the resident unit exercises an ultimate veto power over anything transpiring under its stated or even implied auspices; in other institutions extension has virtual autonomy. Where lines of communication are good, conflicts do not arise.

It is in the area of educational services—functional extension—that the matter of internal relations has tended to be relatively unstructured, and yet it is just here that extension most needs intimate association with the research skills and resources of the mother campus.

Research

An intimate knitting together of extension teaching and services with the research activities of the campus might be listed by many as the *sine qua non* of the American university. The extension specialist needs pertinent, timely information. The scientist needs provocative questions. Together they can form a potent team.

Divisive forces. Unfortunately, there are several factors mitigating against extension-research teamwork. First, residence scholars are increasingly occupied with theory-oriented research, rather than with the fact-finding and action-stimulating research that is grist for the extension mill. Administrators and professors alike regard sophisticated investigations "the open sesame to the world of universal scholarship," as Pinner puts it. Deans of residence colleges generally recruit professors whose reputations rest on basic-research abilities or intellectual lineage, without any particular reference to an extension bent. Adept at such contributions as the building of theoretical models, the new arrivals tend to regard with some scorn the applied researches of their older colleagues. Indeed, the higher the qualifications of faculty members, the less they seem to esteem some of the services which have traditionally been performed by the utilitarian university. In the social sciences, particularly, the new professor seems to have a preference for fundamental questions and gross problems, universal in scope, and he shuns what he calls "manhole counting" or "brush-fire fighting." This separation of the residence faculty from immediate public needs has not occurred in spite of the improvement of the faculty, but because of it, Pinner points out. Administrators are caught between their responsibilities to their supporting publics and their esteem for the new men they have fought so hard to win.[28]

Second, the residence scientists willing to perform research that "makes a difference now" are cosmopolitan rather than community oriented. Local and state research to some extent has gone out of style. Professors believe they can advance their careers more surely on the world stage.[29] Hence university faculty are more likely to be giving of their knowledge and energy to Washington and Thailand than to Main Street. Many faculty members are finding private "outside" consultative activities more lucrative than campus teaching or public research. For some the university seems to be becoming more a base of operations than a retreat. As one university president put it, "The question is now, not how do you get the professor out of his ivory tower, but how do you keep him at home!"[30] In a sense what has happened may be that international, federal, and foundation funds have effectively "captured" American universities, in competition with meager state and regional appropriations for problem-oriented research.

Campfires in the night. In many respects the irreplaceable function of the modern university is research. The free university can explore the frontiers of knowledge and understanding without fear or favor. In order to continue to do so, however, the university must constantly explain and relate itself to its constituents. It is extensionists who perform this vital role of interpretation, thereby freeing their residence colleagues for more esoteric pursuits. By buying

---

28 Frank Pinner, "The Crisis of the State Universities: Analysis and Remedies," *The American College,* (ed.) Nevitt Sanford (New York: John Wiley & Sons, Inc., 1962), p. 940.

29 Delbert C. Miller, "Town and Gown," *College and University Journal* (Summer 1963), p. 24.

30 Burch, *op. cit.,* p. 8.

time and space for scholars, extension itself becomes an essential function of the university, if for no other reason. In short, teaching, searching, and serving are not at war with each other. Each function complements the others. To slight one is to dilute all three.

The need is clear: to make extension personnel more effective fact-finders and stimulators by exposing them to theory-oriented research, and to make researchers more disposed to assist in situational problems raised in extension's fields. Extension may eventually have to build into its own structure extension-research personnel, to join those who have traditionally represented extension teaching. Only in this context, as progenitors of productive scholarship as well as of outreach, can extension organizations help fulfill Lowell's classic vision of America—"aglow with universities like a field with campfires of an army on the march."

Administration

Weak administration based on expediency of action; too many administrative controls leading to internal confusion and external embarrassment; unreasonable delay in eliminating conflicts between extension and other operating divisions of the university—these are the somewhat contradictory charges brought by some commentators against university extension.

A demanding task. Certainly it is true that the problems arising from relations with the multiple and often contradictory forces impinging on university extension have made extension administration a hazardous profession. The university extension universe involves many groups, whose interests often make it difficult for them to be objective; yet friendly cooperation must be maintained with and among faculty, students, nonteaching staff, clientele configurations, legislative bodies, governing boards, academic neighbors, the press, and the public at large. University extension has relations with business, labor, and agriculture; with the community of its residence and with the far corners of the commonwealth; with liberal and conservative, rich and poor; with religious and ethnic groups, professional associations, taxpayers' alliances, reform movements, and patriotic organizations; with state and federal bureaus; with public schools and with other colleges. It must try to serve all, yet hamper none. Extension is an adjunct of government, exposed to the political storms by which the control of that government is determined, yet extension must try to remain aloof from politics. Extension is expected to demonstrate, in a manner appropriate to the dignity of the university, the generosity of the university toward its citizenry, yet do so inexpensively. Extension is expected to help advance knowledge, but not to upset accepted ideas; to dispense knowledge, yet also to develop character; to uphold academic standards, yet to educate any aspirant; to be esthetic and idealistic in a thoroughly practical way; to aid the community in the sorting and balancing of relative values—and to help the university win all its football games.[31]

At the helm of this instrumentality, picking his way among reefs, buffeted by cross winds and beset by counter currents, stands the extension director. Whether his division determines its own course or drifts before the forces of the biennial moment is to a considerable degree determined by his administrative ability. To recognize and define adequately the important tasks confronting extension; to divise or select the most satisfactory approaches; to fit these approaches into an over-all program which gives due consideration to both university standards and public needs, to immediate requirements and long-range considerations; and to secure for this program the support of diverse and sometimes antagonistic groups—all this requires considerable adeptness.

Centralized vs. decentralized.   A pervasive administrative question in extension circles is this: Are extension activities to be handled in an essentially decentralized fashion by the respective colleges and departments or more or less centralized through a single office or division? Something about the "multiversity" seems to invite decentralization. By its very nature the university is a loose confederacy of units of varying size, complexity, and purpose, each with its own public. The professional schools, particularly, have a natural affinity for types of extension work. On the other hand, decentralized extension administration introduces problems of duplication of effort or of death by inattention. What is more, decentralized extension may rob the total extension program of a larger sense of public purpose.

---

[31] Maurice Vance, "Charles R. Van Hise," unpublished Ph.D. thesis, The University of Wisconsin, 1952, pp. 178–79.

Broad vs. local. A second related administrative question may be put this way: Should service programs be extended by a pool of transient specialists or should extension assume the role of a locally based adult education agency? More distinctly, should not extension equip itself with full-time representatives residing in every geographic chink? The latter idea is an intriguing one; it stems from agricultural extension's success with the use of county agents. But a moment's reflection leads to reservations about any analogy between the Cooperative Extension Service and an urban extension service. A single such service, designed to deal directly across the board with all families in our exploding urban society, would require an array of agents "probably too numerous to finance or to cope with from the point of view of organization, function, and discipline. Indeed an urban extension service staffed with locally based urban agents on a scale proportionate to the CES suggests the image of a bureaucracy of do-gooders truly terrifying in its potential for mischief."[32] But this is not to say that university extension does not need some teams of specialists residing off campus, reconnoitering the frontiers of living and learning, exploring and testing new ways of relating the intellectual resources of the campus to the needs of the community, and thus strengthening both the life of the land and the vigor of the university.

General extension service vs. cooperative extension service. Where they now exist side by side, perhaps the toughest administrative problem yet faced by extension executives is to develop a viable entente between general extension and agricultural extension. Houle says this is "the major question now confronting university extension; for compelling reasons they can no longer go their separate ways."[33] While general extension and cooperative extension have common ancestors, as the two services have developed they have come to have important differences which vastly complicate bringing them into team harness. Yet the two agencies have much in common. Neither agency is static. With the expansions and modifications within the two extension arms of the university and with the intermixing of rural and urban people, problems, and interests, it has become apparent that increased communication and coordination between these two extension units are essential if the university

---

[32] Bebout, *op. cit.,* p. 6.
[33] Houle, *op. cit.,* p. 20.

is to serve the people of its region effectively. University extension by its very name implies extending the whole university. University leaders must fabricate a new agency, a central arm of the whole university, designed to extend the whole campus; not a swallowing up of one extension unit by another, but the shaping of a comprehensive organization. The most appropriate mechanism for effecting the coordination of general extension and agricultural extension may very well differ from campus to campus, but the problem must be resolved if university extension objectives are to be met efficiently.

Staffing

A creative extension program does not reside in laboratories or libraries or bureaus but in creative minds. The principal task of the extension administrator is to seek out and foster creative thinking. His paramount challenge is to build an extension faculty. It is no easy job. It involves recruiting, training, and motivating—giving the natural leaders the bit, and prodding the laggards.

To make personnel available for extension teaching, adult education, and public service activities, a university employs a variety of arrangements—each with its strengths and weaknesses.

Unbudgeted extension. Much extension work gets done by regular teaching and research personnel in addition to their other duties and with no salary monies specifically allocated to the function. This practice is common in professional schools of the university, where faculty have both personal and institutional relations with a particular clientele. Most commonly, this type of extension work will take the form of informal consultations, although it may include short-term institutes and conferences. Such "unbudgeted" extension, utilizing voluntary experts, may be well-conceived and continuous, or it may be amateurishly executed and sporadic.

Contract extension. A form of unbudgeted extension (from the university's point of view) is the situation in which a public or private agency contracts, through a fee paid to the university, for the services of an individual or group of individuals. Frequently such services will border on applied research, though they may include laying out and conducting a training program. This pattern manifestly projects professors into the community with no burden on the university's exchequer, but contract extension always carries with it the risk of the university losing partial or total control of the nature of the work done.

Part-time informal instruction.   Extension frequently employs for informal classes and services a number of "outside" teachers whose appointments are not subject to residence faculty review and whose qualifications are a demonstrated mastery of a given subject or procedure and a capacity to teach or work with adults. As can be imagined, some of the best and some of the worst extension work is carried on by these *ad hoc* instructors.

Part-time credit instruction.   For courses carrying university credit, extension may engage part-time nonfaculty teachers whose qualifications are subject to review and approval by appropriate university departments. Among urban universities with large evening programs, this practice is widespread. Gowin and Daigneault report from a survey that a large number of able and interested individuals are available for such duty,[34] but residence deans are understandably reluctant to go too far in this direction: "It's a problem of providing a sense of institutional identity, a feeling for our instructional curriculum, an attitude of being one of us, and of time for student counseling."[35]

Over-load basis.   A good deal of extension teaching is done through the employment of regular faculty members on an "overload" basis, for which additional compensation is provided. On the surface this practice has much to recommend it in that it seems to present a ready means of preserving university standards; but there are a number of pitfalls.

Early extension deans searched for people with "a proper viewpoint." They feared "the influence of the old academic spirit" would render extension work "ineffective and practically useless." One said he had never "met a professor who is not in some way opposed to this (extension) movement."[36] The feeling may scarcely have abated. As a matter of fact, the ordinary classroom teacher may not be adept at extension teaching. Most college faculties have to be

---

[34] D. B. Gowin and George H. Daigneault, *The Part-Time College Teacher* (Chicago: Center for the Study of Liberal Education for Adults, 1961), p. 21.

[35] Burch, quoted in *Challenge to the University*, p. 42.

[36] Louis Reber, quoted in Merle Curti and Vernon Carstensen, *The University of Wisconsin: 1848–1935*, Vol. II (Madison, Wis.: The University of Wisconsin Press, 1949), 592.

combed to find scholars who have the stamina and "the intellectual probity and the teaching skill to deal with adult education."[37]

A second pitfall stems from the fact that over-load payments are usually at a rate well below the proper proportion of residence salary levels. This inevitably prompts a cavalier attitude on the part of some professors toward their extension assignments. In correspondence instruction, for example, it is not unknown for the professor's wife or other member of the family actually to correct the study lessons, even though the professor is listed as in charge of the course. Perhaps worst of all, the practice lends an economic yardstick to the charge that extension work is an "academic sideline" and extension workers "second-class citizens."

Split appointments.   Coming into increasing use is the so-called "split appointment" technique, under which official budgetary recognition is given to the fact that a certain proportion of a professor's time is earmarked for extension work, with his residence teaching and research duties being thereby reduced. This approach would seem to be an ideal method of building extension into the structure of the institution; it leaves unanswered at budget-building time the question of how to get a residence dean and an extension director to agree that a particular person does indeed have the broad-gauged qualifications and commitments implicit in the arrangement. Although university professors ostensibly may be paid to do a number of jobs, the worth of their services typically is evaluated on the basis of how they do only one. "The work assignment for which the vast majority of professors are paid is teaching (in residence or in extension). . . . When they are evaluated, however, as candidates either for a vacant position or for promotion, the evaluation is made principally in terms of their research contributions to their disciplines."[38]

Full-time extension.   To produce extension work in quantity, there is probably little question that a full-time extension staff is the ideal solution. It is the quality of that work that becomes suspect. Full-time extensionists run the risk of losing touch with parent schools and colleges, which hold the balance of power in prestige

[37] Lyman Bryson, *Adult Education* (New York: American Book Company, 1936), p. 170.
[38] Theodore Caplow and Reece J. McGee, *The Academic Market-Place* (New York: Basic Books, Inc., 1958), p. 82.

and resources. The surface results may be smaller salary increases and slower promotions. The deeper problem lies in the gulf that can develop between ongoing research on the campus and the transmission of that new knowledge to the hinterlands. Extensionists can become scarcely better informed than their constituents. Yet the success of agricultural extension with a discrete extension organization suggests that ways can be found to prevent the isolation of the full-time extension man from his residence colleagues. The National Agricultural Extension Center for Advanced Study has played an important role in directing research toward such broad problem areas in which Cooperative Extension administrators and supervisors operate.

In-service orientation. In the recruitment and education of its personnel, the Cooperative Extension Service has indeed been diligent in selecting and training a cadre of workers well-oriented to the task of linking soil and seminar. Yet the CES is not without its staffing problems. The CES focus has been on increasing agricultural efficiency. Its people, and the system from which they spring, now find it very difficult to shift gears to meet what the CES itself calls "the dramatic acceleration in the tempo of changes" occurring on the landscape of rural America.[39] Adjustments in the family farm economy, off-farm influences, population tides, rising educational levels, stresses influencing family living, increased demands on natural resources—all such trends emphasize the fact that the CES must have a dynamic program that is constantly being modernized. Programs and procedures appropriate to yesterday are likely to be obsolete tomorrow.[40] Programs cannot be retooled, however, unless the programmers can be retrained and reoriented.

Few general extension divisions have even made a start at in-service training. Some issue handbooks containing procedural regulations and suggestions on how to teach, but anything approaching career education is generally lacking. Tyler recommends a training program that would include both a series of graded experiences in extension work and scheduled time for seminars or other forms of instruction relevant to the problems of extension education in an urban age. Budget provision should be made for internees, for ad-

---

[39] *Scope Report* (Washington, D.C.: American Association of Land-Grant Colleges and State Universities, April, 1948), p. 3.
[40] *Ibid.,* p. 4.

ditional graduate education for staff members, and for participation in a variety of on-the-job experiences.[41]

Curriculum

Building an extension curriculum is a matter of balancing three perspectives:

First, the extension curriculum should accurately reflect the scope and intensity of the university's total resources—intellectual, spiritual, and physical. Second, the extension curriculum should reflect the needs of individuals and groups caught in a complex of explosive change. Third, the extension curriculum should reflect the overweening requirements of society as a whole.

A central problem in successful programming is to identify accurately what people want, think they need, and actually do need, and incorporate these into a realistic, well-organized, and concerted series of forceful activities.[42] The dilemma for the educator is how to reconcile what he sees as a need for preserving the integrity of the subject-matter and the institution, as contrasted with involving people in the kind of educational experiences they see as meaningful.[43] That something of a balance can be achieved, hundreds of successful, reputable extension programs attest.

Critical needs. What are the current critical needs for adult learning? Tyler lists four: the need for study, understanding, and skills in community development and betterment; the need for greater understanding of the international situation and the changes taking place in economic and political affairs; the need for maintaining and advancing the professional competence of doctors, teachers, executives, nurses, farmers, and those in other occupations based on university education; and the need for retraining and education of large numbers whose present jobs will be eliminated by increased automation.[44]

In meeting such needs, it is the whole university that must become involved. Many present extension programs do not adequately

---

[41] See Tyler, *op. cit.,* 135–54.

[42] J. Paul Leagans, "A Concept of Needs," *Journal of Cooperative Extension* (Summer 1964), 90.

[43] Stephen L. Brower, "Dilemma of Adult Educators," *Journal of Cooperative Extension* (Summer 1964), 114.

[44] Tyler, *op. cit.,* p. 147.

recognize that extension should include not only vocational training but also important social and humanistic purposes.[45] "What we need," suggests Margaret Mead, "are human sciences—to educate people how to live in the new world and how to develop social inventions that will make it possible for us to survive."

In its totality, extension outreach must be stronger and more meaningful than its constituent parts. It must rise above the needs of particular segments to serve the goals of a free society. In so doing, it may at times be the center of disturbance. But an inability to withstand the pressures of selfish interests would be the most serious charge that could be brought against the extension movement.

Cooperative planning. If it is to achieve a properly balanced curriculum, extension obviously needs to consult a variety of advisers. Because a university tends to be an esoteric institution committed essentially to an aristocracy of scholarship, some impulses must come from the outside. But to turn program planning over to the clients is equally unfortunate. An early extensionist captured the proper formula when he wrote:

> Voluntary education is under special temptation to reiterate the same subjects over and over again, subjects in which people are already interested. But surely the purpose of education is to multiply the number of subjects in which men take interest; in Wordsworth's phrase, the broader human sensibilities. It is the conjunction of university guidance with popular receptivity that is required. The men who know what there is to know must have a voice in determining the program, along with those who know what they need.[46]

Because extension administrators are typically so busy with ongoing programs, Tyler recommends the establishment of a separate program planning and development staff, funded with some venture capital, that can take the initiative in making feasibility studies, selecting educational objectives, focusing university resources, identifying participants, working out an appropriate sequence of learning experiences, and evaluating results,[47] all in concert with faculty and lay groups.

[45] *Extension Service*, p. 9.
[46] Richard G. Moulton in *Proceedings*, First National University Extension Conference (Madison, Wis., 1915), p. 200.
[47] Tyler, *op. cit.*, pp. 147–53.

Teaching

Programs of extension work too frequently consist of a large number of projects hastily chosen and thrown together into a paper outline; there is a tendency to measure efficiency and progress upon quantitative rather than qualitative scales; inadequate attention is paid to theories of learning, effective teaching materials, and the peculiar needs of adults; extension teachers are "easy markers."[48] All these are typical of the complaints heard at times about extension teaching.

Psychological data demonstrate that an adult *can* learn throughout life. Sociological data suggest that an adult *should* learn throughout life. But educational data indicate that conventional materials, methods, and techniques of instruction as applied to undergraduates must be modified to meet the needs and interests of adults.[49] Some course content requires the use of concepts, generalizations, techniques, and the like that are largely available only in universities. Other things to learn are of a less advanced character and can be carried on effectively by institutions other than the university. In some cases the university's role may largely be in the training of professional people or volunteers to carry on these activities. Over the years, this problem of identifying the learning tasks that properly utilize the talents of university staff members has been faced by agricultural extension, with the result that a wide range of "cooperators" have been developed to participate in the total adult education program. In most general extension divisions the problem has not been worked out satisfactorily.[50]

In response to basic differences between adult and youth learners, extension attempts to capitalize on the adult's motivation by involving him in assessing needs, formulating objectives, designing and conducting learning activities, and evaluating outcomes. Teaching techniques making use of adult experience have come increasingly into use: case problem-solving, role playing, laboratory exercises, various forms of group discussion, and community projects. Unfortunately the majority of teachers of adults still employ

[48] *Extension Service,* p. 11.
[49] Woods and Hammerberg, *op. cit.,* p. 150.
[50] Tyler, *op. cit.,* p. 144ff.

the teacher-planned methods and the transmitter-receiver techniques used in instructing children.[51] The teacher can set the stage, present some of the material, encourage and reward efforts, and so on, but learning is done by the participant, not by the teacher. Hence, effective extension teaching requires teaching attitudes and learning materials with which the adult can work productively.

Here, indeed, is an extension frontier, particularly in the form of achieving the articulation of the various forms of instruction that are now employed in unilateral fashion. Much such experimentation might well be carried on cooperatively among institutions.

Financing

If ever money were the root of all evil, it certainly is in the case of university extension.

General extension is asked to support itself in whole or in part from student or agency fees. The degree of that so-called "self-support" across the country ranges from 99 per cent to 50 per cent, with the average somewhere around 75 per cent. This situation has led inevitably to an invidious skewing of the enterprise. Many classes and programs are arranged on the basis of whether or not they will pay for themselves or even turn a profit, with only a glance at appropriateness and pertinence. Whole categories of the population go unserved because they are incapable of paying the upkeep. Many extension divisions must cater to well-heeled or highly motivated clientele, and thus price themselves out of the market of many of those groups and individuals most in need of continuing education. One university, for example, has in its industrial management institutes four times the annual enrollment that it has in its school for workers. Yet the potential labor audience is forty times the management audience.

Those extension divisions operating resident "continuation centers" are particularly under pressure to break even. The result is that some of these centers have become little but glorified hotel operations, with the university actively soliciting patronage from all manner of societies and organizations for whose conventions and clinics extension plays only a "housekeeping" role.

---

[51] *Adult Education: A New Imperative for Our Times* (New York: Adult Education Association of the U.S.A., 1961), p. 9.

Agricultural extension, on the other hand, is supported entirely by tax monies, be they federal, state, or local, and handsomely at that. These public funds have contributed directly to Cooperative Extension Service accomplishments, but they have likewise contributed to a situation in which a small minority of the population receives a large majority of the services of the typical land-grant university.

Modest user fees would seem as appropriate for adult students as for undergraduate students, particularly where the educational service received is directly related to vocational advancement. It is the proportion of the extension budget represented by those fees that is the question. Most general extension directors would be satisfied with whatever formula obtains for undergraduate instruction on their respective campuses. For private institutions, this might mean that extension work would still have to be largely self-sustaining; but for public institutions, the subsidy from tax monies would approach 70 to 75 per cent.

It is hard to see how, other than through more extensive public support, a national adult education activity can be broad enough and rich enough to serve adequately the individuals and groups with the most pressing educational needs. This message the National University Extension Association has carried to Congress for many sessions to no avail. State legislatures are uneven in their response.

"Money," once said a university president, "is the final factor that determines educational results." Only by expressing its extension mission and extension commitment in dollars and cents can a university expect any implementation. An extension operation funded entirely by user fees results inevitably in undue emphasis on some phases and neglect of others. There is no escape from this fact of life.

External Relations

Viable communications to and from, and working relationships with, individual students, clientele groups, and sister agencies are obviously factors critical to the success of university extension.

General publicity. Commentators on the university extension scene are unanimous in saying that extension must "make clear to many groups the meaning and value of education . . . and point out the availability of specific educational opportunities"[52] by "utilizing to the fullest degree the many publicity methods by which university extension may be promoted."[53] All this is easier said than done. Merely to describe adult education in general, or a specific offering in particular, does not offer to the potential consumer those "reasons why" which modern advertising theory says are essential to stimulating a response. In other words, in Madison Avenue parlance, you have to talk about, not the steak, but the sizzle. Yet it is not at all difficult to offend the sensibilities of residence faculty with what they consider a commercial approach, demeaning to the dignity of the university; even the National University Extension Association has adopted a code of fair practices, which frowns on anything remotely resembling "hard sell." Furthermore, the costs of promotion are considerable. Nonetheless the typical extension operation devotes considerable time, talent, and money to product publicity through a wide variety of media.

Where costs of instruction must be covered by student fees, recruitment of sufficient "customers" becomes necessary because a small nucleus of interested persons cannot usually provide all the needed financial support. Even in the case of tax-supported programs, universities consider it their obligation to advertise adult offerings as widely as possible so that all citizens who desire to learn will know about the opportunity.

Classes are announced and promoted in a variety of ways. Sometimes a news story is sent to the newspapers and the radio and television stations in an area. Often an announcement or outline of the course is duplicated and distributed. Posters, displays, and exhibits may be used. Hopefully, expenditures for advertising and promotion will be offset by increased income from added enrollment fees, or by increased general interest and support.

There is usually a positive relationship between the number of sources of information and the effects produced. Consideration of a single, "best" channel of information for extension publicity is therefore uneconomical. An important channel of communication is "word-of-mouth." The visible power structure in a community can be influential in this regard, but friends and neighbors are probably more effective.

---

[52] Morton, *op. cit.,* p. 138.
[53] *Extension Service,* p. 93.

People tend to read and learn from sources they identify with. Well-educated young people in white-collar occupations with relatively high income learn more from the mass media than other people do. The greatest single factor relating to the amount of information learned about an extension service is usually the extent of the formal education of the "target."

Participants tend to have more information about an extension program than nonparticipants, they are involved in more interpersonal relations, and they are more likely to have friends or relatives who also participate. In general, the mass media serve to notify and give general information, but at decision time people want to confer with others and gain confidence in the knowledge that those whom they respect concur in their decision to participate.[54]

Liaison. Particularly effective in stimulating public interest and participation is personal liaison with various groups and associations, and this relationship also provides a channel for the flow of felt needs and unverbalized aspirations back to the campus. General extension typically works with existing organizations. Cooperative extension has been adept at uniting local people into special groups. In either approach, too close a relationship may lead to a failure to maintain the objective standards and educational functions of the university. Commercial agencies particularly are apt to try to exploit university services for their own ends.

Mutual aid. Powell tells the story of a good-sized western city, some 50 miles from the state university, where there are adult programs sponsored by a junior college, an evening high school, and a state college:

> "To one of their directors, I said, 'Do you fellows work closely together?'
> " 'You bet we do,' he said; 'we watch each other like dogs.'
> " 'But isn't there something you all collaborate on together?'
> " 'Sure there is. We all work together to keep the university extension division out of here!' "[55]

University extension must establish and retain sound working relationships with other public and private agencies of adult edu-

---

[54] Robert Dick, "How People Learn About an Adult Education Opportunity," The University of Wisconsin Extension Division, undated. Mimeographed.

[55] John Walker Powell, *Learning Comes of Age* (New York: Association Press, 1956), p. 82.

cation, as well as with its own clientele. In many cases, university extension's role is one of "back-stopping" or "reinforcing" the work of other agencies. This enrichment function would be manifestly heightened were there an adequate interchange of information on patterns and plans among all adult education organizations regionally and nationally.

Competition.   General extension has sometimes been so generous and so spineless in its relations with sister agencies that its own integrity has been brought into question. Cooperative extension, by contrast, has developed a self-contained independence which has rendered it of limited usefulness to the three echelons of government that are its joint sponsors. At the national level, the United States Department of Agriculture has found it necessary to develop other field staffs and local committees to advance certain programs. The Soil Conservation Service and the Agricultural Stabilization and Conservation Program, to name only two examples, are in county seats with their own instrumentalities. At the state level, the land-grant universities, unable to utilize county agents for a broad outreach, have attempted to build a variety of other extension mechanisms. Public opinion surveys in Michigan and Illinois indicate the general public does not clearly identify the county agent as a member of the university staff. In North Carolina, less than 40 per cent of the members of the state legislature did so.[56] At the county level, various specialized educational agents are appearing to compete with the Cooperative Extension Service. The resulting proliferation and duplication of effort have so far pretty much resisted any efforts at coordination. Meanwhile the CES complains about the "relentless campaign to convince the public" that it has not lived up to its responsibilities.[57]

Geographic strait-jackets.   Too close an identification with various levels of government has been responsible for the slowness with which some of extension's programs have been effected, and this geographic strait-jacket threatens to be even more restrictive in the years ahead. Municipal universities find themselves hedged in by boundaries that delineate tax districts but not people and their prob-

---

56 T. C. Blalock, "What Legislators Think of Extension," *Journal of Cooperative Extension* (Summer 1964), p. 76.

57 Edward Danforth Eddy, Jr., *Colleges for Our Land and Time* (New York: Harper & Row, Publishers, 1957), p. 239.

lems. State universities have trouble crossing geographic lines that have relevance to traditional politics but not to modern stresses. Cooperative Extension, particularly, is in trouble. The American county is the creature of an engineer's map, laid out to facilitate matters of survey and land description. It has never been a viable delineation in terms of concerns like watershed management, and it is becoming less and less pertinent to the distribution of people and their societal concerns. Yet the CES is wedded to a seemingly inviolable link with county-oriented committees.

There are problems attendant on external relations, but it is those relations that are essential if that anomaly in a free society—the closed community of scholars—is to be wiped out.

Summary

To a greater or lesser degree, American universities accept the extension function. In so doing they are attempting, formally for the first time, to reconcile some of the divergent purposes of academic and everyday life and particularly to bring practical and theoretical considerations into useful, acceptable relationship. This may well be extension's "greatest and most durable social value."[58]

A university is dedicated to the fulfillment of the American dream —as a country where every man has an equal right to achieve inequality and a common right to think uncommon thoughts. Where the ten critical factors are present in university extension, the poet, the artisan, the farmer, the industrialist, the philosopher, the artist, the businessman can study and work together in mutual respect to make the American dream ever more attainable.

---

[58] Creese, *op. cit.,* p. 56.

CHAPTER V

Azimuths

University extension has become a mechanism by which American institutions of higher education—and in a larger sense, the people themselves—seek to extend the resources of the university to all citizens, to extend education throughout the whole period of life, and to extend university concerns to all the vital interests of life. In its broadest application university extension has two guiding principles: first, that the mission of extension is to help lift the individual and collective life of people to higher planes; and second, that in so doing, extension is not necessarily bound by any prior theories as to the structure or nature of a university, but rather that the university and its extension arms will try to undertake any educational task which lies undone and which the university can do and do well.[1]

Today America and her university extension movement face new opportunities. Within the lifetime of most Americans, changes of dramatic speed and scope are exerting a profound effect on American society. Against this backdrop of explosive change, university extension can have its finest hour.

The Climate Today

The American population has expanded from 131 million in 1940 to over 180 million in the 1960's. A restless people always on the move, Americans have forsaken their rural past for city and suburb. The value of the goods and services they produce has nearly doubled, and the bonanza is more equitably distributed.[2]

People. Among the striking post-World War II American phenomena is an explosive birth rate. In the five years between 1950 and 1956 twice as many babies were born as in the whole of the

---

[1] L. H. Adolfson, *Symposium: General University Extension* (University Park, Pa. The Pennsylvania State University, 1960), p. 77.

[2] For a lively summary of the period, see Walter Johnson, *1600 Pennsylvania Avenue, Presidents and People* (Boston: Little, Brown & Co., 1960), pp. 262–64, 266–68.

1930's. People are living longer; the average life expectancy is approaching 70 years. Illiteracy is disappearing. A high school education is within grasp of all and attained by most. College graduates in the population show striking increases in numbers. At least one out of every five adult Americans tries systematically to learn something each year. The growth in total population, in life expectancy, and in the habit of learning suggests that "America is likely to experience an adult education explosion within the next decades."[3]

Place. Major shifts are occurring in the location of the mushrooming American population. From both the rural open country and the central city, people are rushing to vast new complexes of suburbia. Between 1950 and 1960 the metropolitan areas of the country accounted for well over 90 per cent of the total national population growth. The suburbs grew nearly eight times faster than the central cities. Beginning in 1947 over a million white- and blue-collar workers a year fled to the suburbs. By the 1960's, with some fifty million Americans living in the suburbs, the suburbanite approximated the so-called "average American."[4]

This major movement toward city sprawl has produced a need for new kinds of educational programs concerned directly with what can only be described as a bewildering array of problems associated with the process of urbanization: health, housing, urban renewal, building regulation, open space development, merchandising, land-use planning, major public works or improvements, communication, parks, police, schools, traffic, water supply, sanitation, labor-management relations, municipal fiscal duties, and so on. The vast majority of social problems "are correlates, concomitants, or consequences of urban-industrialism. Even the ubiquitous social problems present themselves in more complicated form in the context of suburbia."[5]

The central city is becoming more and more a problem area, choked by congestion and blight. The sprawling outlying area is a gray blur of conformity. Political boundaries have no relation to the public works and welfare stresses that result from galloping

[3] *Volunteers for Learning* (Chicago: National Opinion Research Center, University of Chicago, 1963), p. 3.

[4] Johnson, *op. cit.*

[5] Leo F. Schnore, "Social Problems in an Urban-Industrial Context," *Social Problems* (Winter 1961–62), p. 230.

"interurbanitis." Megalopolis becomes a complex of conflicting objectives, activities, values, and cultures. City has moved to country, country to city. Out of all this emerges a maze.[6]

Nor are all the problems reserved for the new "tension zone" between what was once open country and central city. In terms of land area, *most* of America is losing population. The stresses of adjusting to a declining population, while less dramatic, are no less real than those of adjusting to an increasing number of people.

Urbanization has caught the university world ill-prepared. Universities have neglected the study of social processes that create cities.[7] A compelling research theory is lacking.[8] Urban extension goals are unclear, a fact which is closely related to the lack of common objectives in metropolitan regions themselves, most of which are characterized by a debilitating diffusion in their decision-making processes,[9] and decreased rates of participation on the part of the rank-and-file citizenry.[10]

Physical technology. Urbanization has been accompanied, if indeed not caused, by large-scale technological changes. A continuing revolution in agriculture is being marked by a decline in the number of independent farms and the number of persons employed in agriculture. A continuing revolution in science and industry is being marked by goods and services increasing not by simple addition but by geometric progression, by mass marketing, plentiful power, an abundance of raw materials, speed-ups in transportation and communications, new tools of research. Such changes have modified in a fundamental way the traditional life patterns of American citizens, and the end of these changes is not even remotely in sight.

This vast technological revolution brings with it unprecedented demands for new professions, new jobs, new skills, training, in-

---

6 Herman Berkman, *Our Urban Plant* (Madison, Wis.: The University of Wisconsin Extension Division, 1964), p. 8.

7 Eric E. Lampard, "American Historians and the Study of Urbanization," *The American Historical Review* (October 1961), p. 49.

8 Robert Gertman, "Urban Studies as a Field of Research," *The American Behavioral Scientist* (February 1963), p. 12.

9 Robert C. Wood, "Urban Regions," *Planning 1962* (Chicago: American Society of Planning Officials, 1962), p. 9.

10 Douglas G. Marshall, *Wisconsin's Population*, Agricultural Experiment Statistic Research Bulletin 241 (Madison, Wis.: The University of Wisconsin Press, 1963), p. 5.

sights, understandings. Knowledge of the physical world is doubling every fifteen years. Ninety per cent of the prescriptions written by doctors today could not have been written ten years ago.[11] In Margaret Mead's pungent words, the country is now at the point where "we must educate people in what nobody knew yesterday, and prepare people for what no one knows yet but what some people must know tomorrow."

Social technology.   America is in the throes of "galloping capitalism." A driving energy, a propensity to take risks, increased productivity, a huge consumer demand, business investments in capital equipment, increased governmental expenditures, an almost fanatic pursuit of the trappings of happiness, a world market—all these contribute to boom conditions. The times seem almost unbelievable to many of the depression generation. Even that perpetual complainer, *The Nation,* writes about "Perpetual Prosperity."[12]

The enormous increase in the wealth of the country expresses itself in, among other things, a growing nationalization in American life. The automobile, the airplane, motion pictures, radio, television, and cosmopolitan mail-order catalogs all contribute to the diminution of regional differences. At the same time, a dramatic shift has occurred in the dispersion of wealth, with the lower 95 per cent of the population gaining a larger share of a steadily growing pie. The average American middle-income consumer, says *Fortune,* is not a small landlord or drugstore proprietor; "if any stereotype is at all meaningful, he is a machinist in Detroit."[13] Factory workers drive big cars and even bigger boats, invest in the stock market, and take off regularly for long weekends at lakeshore retreats.

Some of its wealth America gives away or lends overseas in a Good Samaritan role unprecedented in history. The foreign aid program is big enough to prompt perennial charges that it is bankrupting the country, but *Newsweek* has estimated that the percentage of the national product that goes into international assistance is actually less than the amount Americans spend manicuring their lawns.

Catastrophe.   In spite of prosperity, the times can hardly be

---

11 Phillip H. Coombs, in *The Changing University* (Chicago: Center for the Study of Liberal Education for Adults, 1959), p. 25.

12 Johnson, *op. cit.*

13 *Ibid.*

termed utopian. Hanging like a storm cloud on the horizon is the rise of Russia and China as great world powers, inimical to American interests. Yesterday the world was dominated by friendly allies. Now two great civilizations are dedicated to the domination of the world by an alien system. The national purpose in the United States has thus changed from a preoccupation with internal affairs to one of insuring the country's survival. Atom and hydrogen bombs, guided missiles, thermonuclear warheads, airborne destruction of unparalleled quantity has changed the protective quality of the oceans. Where once the nation had nothing to fear but fear itself, today its fears have taken on flesh and metal. The interdependence of the so-called Western nations and the cultivation of the so-called uncommitted countries are no longer merely a humanistic dream; they are a necessity.

There are clouds at home, as well: too many automobile accidents, still too many marginal-income families, too many slums, too tense racial situations, too few good schools and capable teachers, too few hospitals and too little medical care at reasonable cost, too many government instrumentalities in some places and not enough in others[14]—all the symptoms of what has been called the "misdevelopment" of America. As John Kenneth Galbraith protests, the American preoccupation with high and mounting production of *private* goods has resulted in a serious shortage in the production of *public* service.[15] Even the new-found leisure is a threat as well as a boon. Tens of millions of adults feel some dissatisfaction with the ways they are using the hours and days that fly inexorably by. They yearn for immortality, yet they do not know how to spend a rainy Sunday afternoon.[16]

The universities themselves are implicated. The professional school, abetted by the graduate school, is squeezing out liberal education, says Barzun: "The student is not addressed as a person or citizen but only as that dreadful model of our age—the member of society who must be clothed in qualifications and armed with

---

14 *Ibid.*

15 John Kenneth Galbraith, *The Affluent Society* (Boston: Houghton Mifflin Company, 1958).

16 Robert Blakely, *Adult Education In and For a Free Society* (East Lansing, Mich.: "The Fund for Adult Education, 1952), p. 12.

licenses to practice."[17] Extension directors warn their colleagues about an over-emphasis on quantitative counts of "contacts" to the neglect of qualitative measures of actual contributions.[18] A Michigan study says universities and colleges are giving only a casual partnership in any case involving economic decisions in the community. No university has proposed and tested a major approach to the problem of unemployment or unemployability. No single body of scholars in an embattled state has yet succeeded in implementing a dramatic approach to the education of the Negro.[19]

Wishes and ideas. While it is difficult to characterize the desires and needs and values of each American, it appears to be true that a thin and impotent mood dominated the country in the decade before 1960. "The hallmark of the fifties," writes Arthur Schlesinger, Jr., "was a belief that what is good for one's private interest is good for all. Charles E. Wilson gave this idea classic formulation when he suggested that what was good for General Motors was good for the country. And many critics of Wilson seemed to object less to the principle of Wilson's law than to his choice of beneficiary."[20]

But, believes Schlesinger, new forces, new energies, new standards are now straining for expression and release: "People won't fool themselves indefinitely into supposing that the national interest is only the extension of whatever serves their own power and pocket book. . . . If the hallmark of the fifties was the belief in the sanctity of private interests, the hallmark of the sixties may well be the revival of a sense of the supremacy of the public interest."[21]

The new spirit is finding expression in many forms—in and out of the university. With all the bigness and the newness of change, there is growing a pervasive sense of the heightened need for people to understand themselves, their fellow men, their inheritance, their destiny, and their God. The vastly greater interdependence of people, regions, and nations, the attrition of conventional frontiers

---

[17] Jacques Barzun, "The Liberal Arts: Dead or Dying?" *College and University Journal* (Spring 1964), p. 24.

[18] Henry Ahlgren, quoted in *The Milwaukee (Wisconsin) Journal,* October 16, 1963, p. 1.

[19] Francis C. Pray, "Order, Wealth, and Knowledge," *College and University Journal* (Spring 1964), p. 6.

[20] Arthur Schlesinger, Jr., "The New Mood in Politics," *Esquire* (January 1961), p. 58.

[21] *Ibid.,* p. 6.

and the emergence of others even more intriguing, the ever-perplex-
ing adjustment of multiplying man and disappearing land, relative
economic stability at an unprecedented level of general prosperity,
the steady pressure on the voter to render sound economic, and even
scientific, judgments—these qualitative shifts in the American challenge are leading more and more Americans to ask some pivotal
questions: What is at the heart of American civilization? What are
the values that give meaning? Toward what star is the society oriented? And the answer that is coming back is that "freedom is not
an end in itself. Freedom is a means to an end. The role of freedom
is to help people become the best that they are capable of."[22]

This, people are discovering, or rediscovering, is the essence of
the American idea. The American is not to be trained merely to
become an efficient economic cog; he is not to be indoctrinated to
march in lockstep. "The explosive in democracy is the infectious
conviction that the individual does not have to accept his lot passively, that it can, in part at least, be man-altered, and that *he* can
take part in altering it."[23]

To alter the environment, to find panaceas for individual freedom
and progress, Americans have tried different approaches. They are
still trying them. Some people tend to think that if business is let
alone, everything will work out because there will be plenty of
money for everyone, and that will solve all the problems. Others
tend to consider knowledge as sufficient for its own sake, and feel
that if people are educated enough all other problems will be easily
solved. Still others tend to think any problem can be solved by
passing a regulation or setting up a government bureau.[24] If any
mood characterizes the sixties, it is the belief that all three approaches are needed, that they are not mutually exclusive nor
necessarily competitive, but that, working in harness, the private
sector, education, and government can realize the best hope of earth.

The universities are interpreting the new sensibilities of the sixties
in a number of ways. First, they are groping toward an acceptance
of the responsibility of seeing that knowledge and skills which
scholars have developed or assembled are taken into the field where
they can be used to affect urban-industrial change and development

---

[22] Blakely, in *The Changing University,* p. 56.
[23] Blakely, *Adult Education,* p. 4.
[24] See Pray, *op. cit.*

and help people live a better life in such a society[25]—in substance, to help make democracy work in its new surroundings.

Second, universities are recognizing that skills obsolesce, facts wear out, and that what is worth learning is mainly the knack of learning itself. To be practical, an education now must prepare a man for work that doesn't yet exist and whose nature can't even be imagined. This can be done only by teaching people how to learn, by giving them the kind of intellectual discipline and the depth of understanding that will enable them to apply man's accumulated wisdom to new conditions as they arise.[26] While not neglecting conventional technical training which stresses a tangible salable skill, adult educators particularly are seeking to provide education that cultivates reasoning ability, creativity, tolerance, eagerness for new ideas, a sense of history, and faith in the potentialities of the future.

And third, universities see it as requisite to provide educational opportunities for people who will become leaders for the *public* good; not just for the good of corporations, not just for the good of agriculture, not just for the good of professions, but in terms of the commonweal.[27]

Given an army of adult educators with this sort of perspective, the whole country will share in the higher energy they generate, and more and more Americans will be able to say, like Richter, the German novelist known as "Jean Paul": "I have made as much out of myself as could be made of the stuff."[28]

Personality.   There are no giants in the earth in adult education these days, or so it would seem; no four-star generals like Harper and Van Hise. But there is a growing cadre of lieutenants. Indeed, Blakely likens their role to that of the "regulars" in the United States Armed Forces—the 200,000 forgotten men of 1939 who five years later had trained 14 million civilians and led them to victory around the world. The country has today, he says, a citizen-army ready for recruitment into adult education—"those who care, who worry, who

---

[25] John E. Bebout, "The Idea of the Urban Extension Service" (New Brunswick, N.J.: Rutgers—The State University, January 1963), p. 1. Mimeograph.

[26] Charles E. Silberman, "The Remaking of American Education," *Fortune* (June 1961), p. 55.

[27] Blakely, in *The Changing University,* p. 59.

[28] "Adult Learning Is Necessary," *The Royal Bank of Canada Monthly Letter* (October 1963), p. 4.

are concerned, who think, who are tired of being afraid and self-seeking. They are being asked . . . to come alive. We have today the 'moral equivalent of war,' the growing awareness that to save and improve our free way of life we must exemplify it."

To each extension educator Blakely says "each of us is the individual whom our society exists to serve; and each of us is the instrument to advance the kind of society which exists to serve the individual."[29]

Not all adult educators are or should be employed by university extension. As Fischer has pointed out, in the last half century a whole network of services has come into existence to do many of the things only colleges were in a position to undertake at the turn of the century.[30] If the expression "cooperative extension" had not long ago been preempted, somebody would by this time have invented it and applied it to an enterprise called urban extension, Bebout suggests. He speculates the next few years will see a substantial increase in the number of persons who might be described as "urban agents"; only a few of them, however, may be on the university staff: the urban adjustment agent, the community development agent, the neighborhood civic secretary, the area coordinator, the urban extension specialist, and the general urban agent. It will be the university's principal task, Bebout feels, to provide the same kind of "communication and brokerage service" between the university and the urban community as that achieved by agricultural agents, with local governments and private industry gradually employing more and more people in staff positions to supplement the work of university-employed extensionists.[31]

Whatever pattern emerges, Blakely urges that today's university extension educators start, each with himself and all with each other, to ask the right questions: "What is adult education trying to do? In terms of the free individual and the free society, in terms of the central issues of our time, why is it important?"[32]

29 Blakely, *Adult Education*, pp. 12–13.
30 John H. Fischer, quoted in "The Remaking of American Education," p. 55.
31 Bebout, *op. cit.*, p. 72.
32 Blakely, *Adult Education*, p. 14.

The Challenge of Change

The preceding examination of the American climate suggests that the country is moving into a period in which both the need and the demand for life-long learning will become more and more insistent on the part of more and more Americans, and that there are a number of specific factors at work which dictate a dramatic growth in university extension activities particularly.

Stimulus. These stimulating factors may be summarized as:

1. The international crisis and the technological revolution, both of which bring unheralded demands for new knowledge, skills, and insights on the part of citizens. People will turn to many educational agencies, but particularly to the colleges and universities, with their growing reservoir of educational resources.

2. The growth in total population, in life expectancy, and in educational levels, which account for a vastly increasing number of adults who constitute a "market" for university extension services.

3. The major movement of population from farm to city, with accompanying needs for new kinds of extension programs concerned with urban renewal and suburban development, based upon research.

4. A continuing upswing in the standard of living and in the amount of leisure available to more and more Americans, giving those citizens both the money and the time to engage in learning experiences of quality.

5. The cumulative impact of the depression, World War II, and the Korean conflict in orienting adults toward seeking educational services on college campuses, and in orienting faculties toward providing adult-education programs.

6. A steady increase in the number of voluntary associations, with their growing need for back-stopping in the areas of leadership training, educational materials, and expert consultation.

Response. The university extension concept has never been uniform. Flexner declared that "universities must at all times give society, not what society wants, but what it needs."[33] Butts replied that "it is idle to try to prove to people that they ought to prefer a (university) system that they unquestionably do not like."[34] This book has argued for balance between responsibility for academic standards and responsiveness to public needs. In that context, the

---

[33] Abraham Flexner, *Universities—American, English, German* (New York: Oxford University Press, Inc., 1930), p. 15.

[34] Freeman Butts, *The College Charts Its Course* (New York: McGraw-Hill Book Company, 1939), p. 191.

challenge to university extension is clear. Each university will have "its own approach, its own evolution, its own role it can best play in preparing our citizenry for whatever lies ahead. Based upon its own institutional organization, its own problems, its own history, each has an indigenous contribution to make."[35]

Extension teaching. Adults are returning to school in America in striking numbers. Schooling, once an accepted occupation for the young only, has become a socially recognized adult avocation. The concept of formal education as a terminal activity confined to man's pre-adult years is slowly giving way to the notion that it should be a continuing resource available in the adult years as well. The image of the self-made leader of men who succeeded in spite of limited schooling has been replaced by the ideal of the university-trained executive who is continuing his education. Whatever a man's motivation—whether he is seeking to improve himself in his job, catch up on missed opportunities for degrees or diplomas, pursue a hobby or a new-found interest, satisfy intellectual curiosity, develop esthetic sensibilities, become a more informed participating citizen, find personal purpose in a world that seems to have passed men by, have intellectual companionship, overcome the boredom of increasing leisure, or even, as some cynics suspect, find a haven that's warm, congenial, and away from the nagging problems of home and office—within reach there are an infinite variety of courses, conferences, and clinics where he can hope to satisfy his needs.[36] Among the agencies of American society providing such learning experiences is university extension.

Extension services. Just as they turn to the university for individual enrichment, so are people turning to their universities for help in what Eric Sevareid has called "America's misdevelopment" —chronic insecurity for many farmers and a malignant tumor in the federal budget . . . too many airlines . . . a desperate need for railroad transit . . . the monstrous social sprawl called the megalopolis, which is neither city nor country and is governed by up to a hundred overlapping units of government, meaning the communities are not governed at all but merely administered . . . millions of our poorest, most unskilled people in the Harlems of the country, where

---

[35] Berkman, *op. cit.,* p. 59.
[36] Marc Belth and Herbert Schaeler, *Liberal Education for Adults Re-Examined* (Chicago: Center for the Study of Liberal Education for Adults, 1959), pp. 1–2.

relief and schooling facilities break down, tensions build up alarmingly, and jobs for the young are not to be found . . . the spread of automation, all under an umbrella of persistent international tension.

These issues touch the life of every individual with a penetrating intimacy: How harassing is his trip to work, how fruitful are his home surroundings, will the value of his house and property change, are his wife and family adequately protected, are the children receiving a good education, is he keeping abreast of vocational changes, is he paying a fair share of the costs of government or is the bill distributed unequally, how does he get unslanted news of the world, where can he go for a picnic or a fishing trip, will his sewer back up again next year, will his water turn rusty?

University extension increasingly is being asked to serve as a catalyst in the community, to act as a bridge between the community and the university as a whole, to develop liaison with other agencies working in the field, to stimulate and sometimes perform both basic and applied research, to provide teaching and consulting services— in short, to make certain that the unique resources of the American university are applied where most needed in an alliance for American progress.[37]

Education for the new leisure. Edward Crafts says a new age of leisure is almost here. Material needs are satisfied with less and less effort. Marginal chores are getting done with time to spare. The leisure hours just around the corner are uncommitted hours.[38]

In this new era, in which men are now potentially freed from the grinding necessities, education becomes an end, just as it was for the "liberal" man of ancient Greece—literally the liberated man, the nonslave. The Greeks equated leisure, freemen, and education. The Greek word for school was derived from the word for leisure. Only free men had leisure, and hence schooling. By substituting the machine for the slave, modern technology at last is saying that all men can be free; America's conscience says men should have education worthy of their freedom.

As the country enters a whole new era of human stress and en-

---

[37] *Report of the Policy Statement Committee* (Washington, D.C.: National University Extension Association, 1961), p. 10.

[38] Edward Crafts, "The Time Is Now," Paper presented before 28th annual meeting of National Wildlife Federation, Las Vegas, Nevada, March 6, 1964, p. 2.

deavor, education is no longer merely a matter of survival; it becomes the wellspring of the pursuit of meaning and of happiness. As people are freed of vocational duress, as they become increasingly a leisure class, education—the search for truth—becomes the touchstone for determining what the quality of that leisure shall be.

Education for democracy. Education is the handmaiden of democracy. The general franchise requires an enlightened people. The educational system has evolved from the simplest forms and youngest people up a ladder to adult education, education through university extension. A national consensus is coming to view an education not as a preparation for life but as an intimate part of life. In these times the door is being opened to a crucial concept— education as a lifetime pursuit.

Education supports democracy. At the same time that the American people were establishing a democracy, they were building a country, pushing back physical frontiers, exploiting resources; and education reflected these requirements. Now Americans are refining democracy and developing people. Today's education must reflect this new focus.

Toward the great society. Speaking on the Irvine campus of the University of California in June of 1964, President Lyndon B. Johnson asked, "Why not an urban extension service, operated by universities across the country and similar to the agricultural extension service that assists rural areas?" As America moves rapidly toward urbanization, President Johnson's question takes on striking significance. In any drive toward the "great society," creating opportunity for continuing learning, training, and community development becomes a national imperative. Fifty years ago the Cooperative Extension Service helped revolutionize agricultural life. Today a broadly conceived urban extension program could help transform life in the cities and towns of America. Through its state universities, land-grant colleges, and other institutions of higher education, the United States has the existing personnel and machinery to bring vast benefits to millions of Americans. The basic prerequisite is adequate funding.

A first-rate urban extension service would require at least as much federal support as that now given to agricultural extension—something like $75 million a year, with the states making matching appropriations. There are reasons for federal investment. First, state

and local financial resources are already strained to the utmost to
keep pace with mounting demands for on-campus instruction.
Second, because university general extension must now be self-
supporting to a heavy degree, student fees effectively price out of
the market many of those individuals and groups most in need of
services. Third, urbanization is clearly a national problem and a
national opportunity. In short, the experience in agriculture demon-
strates that only with federal support will a university extension
program have the depth and breadth to do the job that needs doing.

The instrument for effecting control of program planning and
implementation might be a series of comprehensive state plans
developed by designated universities or state boards in concert with
local people, and reviewed by the United States Office of Education
under the guidance of a coordinating committee composed of representatives of those federal cabinet agencies with a stake in urban
extension. Such state-wide planning would give great leeway to
each state to work out its own destiny, employing the resources of
all appropriate educational institutions within its boundaries. At the
same time a federal review would assure adequate nation-wide
coordination.

A comprehensive urban extension program would improve America's educational system, create a better-informed electorate, increase
the productivity of workers, enhance cultural appreciations, and
prepare millions of citizens to meet the new challenges of a rapidly
changing technological society with an increasingly urban focus.

Getting things moving.   Down a wilderness trail in the Adiron-
dack Mountains in September of 1901 a rattletrap buckboard
jolted through the night, skidding off ruts, swaying past boulders,
the horses almost out of control. The passenger sat tensed and
hunched, eyes screwed up behind steel-rimmed spectacles, mouth
clenched tight beneath a prairie-dry mustache, his thoughts projected far out across a new century big with change. "Too fast?" the
driver shouted. Theodore Roosevelt, Vice-President of the United
States and due before dawn to become President, rattled back like
a Gatling gun: "Go ahead . . . Go on . . . Go on!"[39]

It was Teddy Roosevelt who set the tone and pace for a day that
saw the first flowering of university extension. In like manner it was

---

[39] *Time*, March 3, 1958, p. 16.

John F. Kennedy, speaking in Boston on the eve of his election in 1960, who expressed the spirit of a new era. Leaders must, he said, continually "set before the American people the unfinished business of society."

For the propounding of this American agenda there are many agencies—public and private, federal and local, commercial and educational. None is more objective than the university. None is better motivated than a university with an unswerving commitment to university extension. None is better equipped than a university extension organization charged with facing "unfinished business." It is university extension that again can say to America: "Go ahead . . . go on!"

Bibliography

Adolfson, L. H., "Extension Theory and Practice," *Proceedings of the National University Extension Association,* 1945.

Bebout, John E., "The Idea of the Urban Extension Service." New Brunswick: Rutgers—The State University, January, 1963. mimeograph.

Blakely, Robert, *Adult Education In and For a Free Society.* East Lansing, Mich.: The Fund for Adult Education, 1952.

Bryson, Lyman, *Adult Education.* New York: American Book Co., 1936.

Burch, Glen, *Challenge to the University.* Chicago: Center for the Study of Liberal Education for Adults, 1961.

Creese, James, *The Extension of University Teaching.* New York: American Association of Adult Education, 1941.

Eddy, Edward Danforth, Jr., *Colleges for Our Land and Time.* New York: Harper & Row, Publishers, 1957.

Houle, Cyril, *Major Trends in Higher Adult Education.* Chicago: Center for the Study of Liberal Education for Adults, 1959.

Kelsey, Lincoln David, and Connor Chiles Hearne, *Cooperative Extension Work,* (3rd ed.). Ithaca, N.Y.: Comstock Publishing Associates, 1963.

Knowles, Malcom S., "Adult Education in the United States," *Adult Education* (Winter 1955).

Liveright, A. A., *Adult Education in Colleges and Universities.* Chicago: Center for the Study of Liberal Education for Adults, 1960.

Morton, John R., *University Extension in the United States.* Birmingham, Ala.: University of Alabama Press, 1953.

Petersen, Renee and William, *University Adult Education.* New York: Harper & Row, Publishers, 1960.

Powell, John Walker, *Learning Comes of Age.* New York: Association Press, 1956.

Proceedings of the Association of State Universities and Land-Grant Colleges, 1961.

Proceedings of the First National University Extension Conference. Madison, Wis., 1915.

Report of the Policy Statement Committee, Washington, D.C., The National University Extension Association, n.d.

"Scope Report." Washington, D.C.: American Association of State Universities and Land-Grant Colleges, April, 1958.

"The Contemporary University: U.S.A.," *Daedalus* (Fall 1964).

Today's Critical Needs and University Extension. Washington, D.C.: Division of General Extension, American Association of State Universities and Land-Grant Colleges, 1961.

True, Alfred Charles, *A History of Agricultural Extension Work in the United States,* United States Department of Agriculture Bulletin No. 15. Washington, D.C.: Government Printing Office, 1928.

Verner, Coolie, and Alan Booth, *Adult Education.* New York: The Center for Applied Research in Education, 1964.

Volunteers for Learning. Chicago: National Opinion Research Center, University of Chicago, 1963.

Woods, Baldwin, and Helen Hammerberg, "University Extension Education in the United States," *Universities in Adult Education.* Paris: UNESCO, 1952.

Index

Index